Mometrix
TEST PREPARATION

MW00561904

Keystone
Algebra I EOC
Success Strategies

DEAR FUTURE EXAM SUCCESS STORY

First of all, **THANK YOU** for purchasing Mometrix study materials!

Second, congratulations! You are one of the few determined test-takers who are committed to doing whatever it takes to excel on your exam. **You have come to the right place.** We developed these study materials with one goal in mind: to deliver you the information you need in a format that's concise and easy to use.

In addition to optimizing your guide for the content of the test, we've outlined our recommended steps for breaking down the preparation process into small, attainable goals so you can make sure you stay on track.

We've also analyzed the entire test-taking process, identifying the most common pitfalls and showing how you can overcome them and be ready for any curveball the test throws you.

Standardized testing is one of the biggest obstacles on your road to success, which only increases the importance of doing well in the high-pressure, high-stakes environment of test day. Your results on this test could have a significant impact on your future, and this guide provides the information and practical advice to help you achieve your full potential on test day.

Your success is our success

We would love to hear from you! If you would like to share the story of your exam success or if you have any questions or comments in regard to our products, please contact us at **800-673-8175** or **support@mometrix.com**.

Thanks again for your business and we wish you continued success!

Sincerely,
The Mometrix Test Preparation Team

TABLE OF CONTENTS

INTRODUCTION _____ 1

STRATEGY #1 – PLAN BIG, STUDY SMALL _____ 2

STRATEGY #2 – MAKE YOUR STUDYING COUNT _____ 3

STRATEGY #3 – PRACTICE THE RIGHT WAY _____ 4

STRATEGY #4 – PACE YOURSELF _____ 6

TEST-TAKING STRATEGIES _____ 7

OPERATIONS WITH REAL NUMBERS AND EXPRESSIONS _____ 11
    NUMBER BASICS _____ 11
    RATIONAL NUMBERS _____ 12
    NUMBER LINES _____ 13
    ABSOLUTE VALUE _____ 13
    OPERATIONS _____ 13
    SUBTRACTION WITH REGROUPING _____ 16
    ORDER OF OPERATIONS _____ 17
    PROPERTIES OF EXPONENTS _____ 18
    FACTORS AND MULTIPLES _____ 18
    FRACTIONS, DECIMALS, AND PERCENTAGES _____ 19
    PROPORTIONS AND RATIOS _____ 25
    SLOPE _____ 27
    CROSS MULTIPLICATION _____ 27

OPERATIONS AND LINEAR EQUATIONS AND INEQUALITIES _____ 28
    LINEAR EXPRESSIONS _____ 28
    LINEAR EQUATIONS _____ 28
    SOLVING EQUATIONS _____ 29
    GRAPHING EQUATIONS _____ 34
    INEQUALITIES _____ 35
    SYSTEMS OF EQUATIONS _____ 40
    ADVANCED SYSTEMS OF EQUATIONS _____ 43
    CALCULATIONS USING POINTS _____ 44
    POLYNOMIALS _____ 45
    RATIONAL EXPRESSIONS _____ 48
    QUADRATICS _____ 49

LINEAR FUNCTIONS AND DATA ORGANIZATIONS _____ 52
    ALGEBRAIC THEOREMS _____ 52
    BASIC FUNCTIONS _____ 52
    WORKING WITH FUNCTIONS _____ 58
    ADVANCED FUNCTIONS _____ 60
    SEQUENCES _____ 63
    ADVANCED SEQUENCES AND SERIES _____ 65
    PROBABILITY _____ 67
    PERMUTATIONS AND COMBINATIONS IN PROBABILITY _____ 71

Tree Diagrams _____ 72
Two-Way Frequency Tables _____ 73
Expected Value _____ 73
Data Analysis _____ 74
Measures of Central Tendency _____ 77
Displaying Information _____ 79
Scatter Plots _____ 85

Keystone Practice Test #1 _____ 87

Answer Key and Explanations for Test #1 _____ 102

Keystone Practice Test #2 _____ 112

Answer Key and Explanations for Test #2 _____ 129

How to Overcome Test Anxiety _____ 135

Additional Bonus Material _____ 141

Introduction

Thank you for purchasing this resource! You have made the choice to prepare yourself for a test that could have a huge impact on your future, and this guide is designed to help you be fully ready for test day. Obviously, it's important to have a solid understanding of the test material, but you also need to be prepared for the unique environment and stressors of the test, so that you can perform to the best of your abilities.

For this purpose, the first section that appears in this guide is the **Success Strategies**. We've devoted countless hours to meticulously researching what works and what doesn't, and we've boiled down our findings to the five most impactful steps you can take to improve your performance on the test. We start at the beginning with study planning and move through the preparation process, all the way to the testing strategies that will help you get the most out of what you know when you're finally sitting in front of the test.

We recommend that you start preparing for your test as far in advance as possible. However, if you've bought this guide as a last-minute study resource and only have a few days before your test, we recommend that you skip over the first two Success Strategies since they address a long-term study plan.

If you struggle with **test anxiety**, we strongly encourage you to check out our recommendations for how you can overcome it. Test anxiety is a formidable foe, but it can be beaten, and we want to make sure you have the tools you need to defeat it.

Strategy #1 – Plan Big, Study Small

There's a lot riding on your performance. If you want to ace this test, you're going to need to keep your skills sharp and the material fresh in your mind. You need a plan that lets you review everything you need to know while still fitting in your schedule. We'll break this strategy down into three categories.

Information Organization

Start with the information you already have: the official test outline. From this, you can make a complete list of all the concepts you need to cover before the test. Organize these concepts into groups that can be studied together, and create a list of any related vocabulary you need to learn so you can brush up on any difficult terms. You'll want to keep this vocabulary list handy once you actually start studying since you may need to add to it along the way.

Time Management

Once you have your set of study concepts, decide how to spread them out over the time you have left before the test. Break your study plan into small, clear goals so you have a manageable task for each day and know exactly what you're doing. Then just focus on one small step at a time. When you manage your time this way, you don't need to spend hours at a time studying. Studying a small block of content for a short period each day helps you retain information better and avoid stressing over how much you have left to do. You can relax knowing that you have a plan to cover everything in time. In order for this strategy to be effective though, you have to start studying early and stick to your schedule. Avoid the exhaustion and futility that comes from last-minute cramming!

Study Environment

The environment you study in has a big impact on your learning. Studying in a coffee shop, while probably more enjoyable, is not likely to be as fruitful as studying in a quiet room. It's important to keep distractions to a minimum. You're only planning to study for a short block of time, so make the most of it. Don't pause to check your phone or get up to find a snack. It's also important to **avoid multitasking**. Research has consistently shown that multitasking will make your studying dramatically less effective. Your study area should also be comfortable and well-lit so you don't have the distraction of straining your eyes or sitting on an uncomfortable chair.

 The time of day you study is also important. You want to be rested and alert. Don't wait until just before bedtime. Study when you'll be most likely to comprehend and remember. Even better, if you know what time of day your test will be, set that time aside for study. That way your brain will be used to working on that subject at that specific time and you'll have a better chance of recalling information.

Finally, it can be helpful to team up with others who are studying for the same test. Your actual studying should be done in as isolated an environment as possible, but the work of organizing the information and setting up the study plan can be divided up. In between study sessions, you can discuss with your teammates the concepts that you're all studying and quiz each other on the details. Just be sure that your teammates are as serious about the test as you are. If you find that your study time is being replaced with social time, you might need to find a new team.

Strategy #2 – Make Your Studying Count

You're devoting a lot of time and effort to preparing for this test, so you want to be absolutely certain it will pay off. This means doing more than just reading the content and hoping you can remember it on test day. It's important to make every minute of study count. There are two main areas you can focus on to make your studying count.

Retention

It doesn't matter how much time you study if you can't remember the material. You need to make sure you are retaining the concepts. To check your retention of the information you're learning, try recalling it at later times with minimal prompting. Try carrying around flashcards and glance at one or two from time to time or ask a friend who's also studying for the test to quiz you.

To enhance your retention, look for ways to put the information into practice so that you can apply it rather than simply recalling it. If you're using the information in practical ways, it will be much easier to remember. Similarly, it helps to solidify a concept in your mind if you're not only reading it to yourself but also explaining it to someone else. Ask a friend to let you teach them about a concept you're a little shaky on (or speak aloud to an imaginary audience if necessary). As you try to summarize, define, give examples, and answer your friend's questions, you'll understand the concepts better and they will stay with you longer. Finally, step back for a big picture view and ask yourself how each piece of information fits with the whole subject. When you link the different concepts together and see them working together as a whole, it's easier to remember the individual components.

Finally, practice showing your work on any multi-step problems, even if you're just studying. Writing out each step you take to solve a problem will help solidify the process in your mind, and you'll be more likely to remember it during the test.

Modality

Modality simply refers to the means or method by which you study. Choosing a study modality that fits your own individual learning style is crucial. No two people learn best in exactly the same way, so it's important to know your strengths and use them to your advantage.

For example, if you learn best by visualization, focus on visualizing a concept in your mind and draw an image or a diagram. Try color-coding your notes, illustrating them, or creating symbols that will trigger your mind to recall a learned concept. If you learn best by hearing or discussing information, find a study partner who learns the same way or read aloud to yourself. Think about how to put the information in your own words. Imagine that you are giving a lecture on the topic and record yourself so you can listen to it later.

For any learning style, flashcards can be helpful. Organize the information so you can take advantage of spare moments to review. Underline key words or phrases. Use different colors for different categories. Mnemonic devices (such as creating a short list in which every item starts with the same letter) can also help with retention. Find what works best for you and use it to store the information in your mind most effectively and easily.

3

Strategy #3 – Practice the Right Way

Your success on test day depends not only on how many hours you put into preparing, but also on whether you prepared the right way. It's good to check along the way to see if your studying is paying off. One of the most effective ways to do this is by taking practice tests to evaluate your progress. Practice tests are useful because they show exactly where you need to improve. Every time you take a practice test, pay special attention to these three groups of questions:

- The questions you got wrong
- The questions you had to guess on, even if you guessed right
- The questions you found difficult or slow to work through

This will show you exactly what your weak areas are, and where you need to devote more study time. Ask yourself why each of these questions gave you trouble. Was it because you didn't understand the material? Was it because you didn't remember the vocabulary? Do you need more repetitions on this type of question to build speed and confidence? Dig into those questions and figure out how you can strengthen your weak areas as you go back to review the material.

 Additionally, many practice tests have a section explaining the answer choices. It can be tempting to read the explanation and think that you now have a good understanding of the concept. However, an explanation likely only covers part of the question's broader context. Even if the explanation makes perfect sense, **go back and investigate** every concept related to the question until you're positive you have a thorough understanding.

As you go along, keep in mind that the practice test is just that: practice. Memorizing these questions and answers will not be very helpful on the actual test because it is unlikely to have any of the same exact questions. If you only know the right answers to the sample questions, you won't be prepared for the real thing. **Study the concepts** until you understand them fully, and then you'll be able to answer any question that shows up on the test.

It's important to wait on the practice tests until you're ready. If you take a test on your first day of study, you may be overwhelmed by the amount of material covered and how much you need to learn. Work up to it gradually.

On test day, you'll need to be prepared for answering questions, managing your time, and using the test-taking strategies you've learned. It's a lot to balance, like a mental marathon that will have a big impact on your future. Like training for a marathon, you'll need to start slowly and work your way up. When test day arrives, you'll be ready.

Start with the strategies you've read in the first two Success Strategies—plan your course and study in the way that works best for you. If you have time, consider using multiple study resources to get different approaches to the same concepts. It can be helpful to see difficult concepts from more than one angle. Then find a good source for practice tests. Many times, the test website will suggest potential study resources or provide sample tests.

Practice Test Strategy

If you're able to find at least three practice tests, we recommend this strategy:

UNTIMED AND OPEN-BOOK PRACTICE

Take the first test with no time constraints and with your notes and study guide handy. Take your time and focus on applying the strategies you've learned.

TIMED AND OPEN-BOOK PRACTICE

Take the second practice test open-book as well, but set a timer and practice pacing yourself to finish in time.

TIMED AND CLOSED-BOOK PRACTICE

Take any other practice tests as if it were test day. Set a timer and put away your study materials. Sit at a table or desk in a quiet room, imagine yourself at the testing center, and answer questions as quickly and accurately as possible.

Keep repeating timed and closed-book tests on a regular basis until you run out of practice tests or it's time for the actual test. Your mind will be ready for the schedule and stress of test day, and you'll be able to focus on recalling the material you've learned.

Strategy #4 – Pace Yourself

Once you're fully prepared for the material on the test, your biggest challenge on test day will be managing your time. Just knowing that the clock is ticking can make you panic even if you have plenty of time left. Work on pacing yourself so you can build confidence against the time constraints of the exam. Pacing is a difficult skill to master, especially in a high-pressure environment, so **practice is vital**.

Set time expectations for your pace based on how much time is available. For example, if a section has 60 questions and the time limit is 30 minutes, you know you have to average 30 seconds or less per question in order to answer them all. Although 30 seconds is the hard limit, set 25 seconds per question as your goal, so you reserve extra time to spend on harder questions. When you budget extra time for the harder questions, you no longer have any reason to stress when those questions take longer to answer.

Don't let this time expectation distract you from working through the test at a calm, steady pace, but keep it in mind so you don't spend too much time on any one question. Recognize that taking extra time on one question you don't understand may keep you from answering two that you do understand later in the test. If your time limit for a question is up and you're still not sure of the answer, mark it and move on, and come back to it later if the time and the test format allow. If the testing format doesn't allow you to return to earlier questions, just make an educated guess; then put it out of your mind and move on.

On the easier questions, be careful not to rush. It may seem wise to hurry through them so you have more time for the challenging ones, but it's not worth missing one if you know the concept and just didn't take the time to read the question fully. Work efficiently but make sure you understand the question and have looked at all of the answer choices, since more than one may seem right at first.

Even if you're paying attention to the time, you may find yourself a little behind at some point. You should speed up to get back on track, but do so wisely. Don't panic; just take a few seconds less on each question until you're caught up. Don't guess without thinking, but do look through the answer choices and eliminate any you know are wrong. If you can get down to two choices, it is often worthwhile to guess from those. Once you've chosen an answer, move on and don't dwell on any that you skipped or had to hurry through. If a question was taking too long, chances are it was one of the harder ones, so you weren't as likely to get it right anyway.

On the other hand, if you find yourself getting ahead of schedule, it may be beneficial to slow down a little. The more quickly you work, the more likely you are to make a careless mistake that will affect your score. You've budgeted time for each question, so don't be afraid to spend that time. Practice an efficient but careful pace to get the most out of the time you have.

6

Test-Taking Strategies

This section contains a list of test-taking strategies that you may find helpful as you work through the test. By taking what you know and applying logical thought, you can maximize your chances of answering any question correctly!

It is very important to realize that every question is different and every person is different: no single strategy will work on every question, and no single strategy will work for every person. That's why we've included all of them here, so you can try them out and determine which ones work best for different types of questions and which ones work best for you.

Question Strategies

⊘ READ CAREFULLY

Read the question and the answer choices carefully. Don't miss the question because you misread the terms. You have plenty of time to read each question thoroughly and make sure you understand what is being asked. Yet a happy medium must be attained, so don't waste too much time. You must read carefully and efficiently.

⊘ CONTEXTUAL CLUES

Look for contextual clues. If the question includes a word you are not familiar with, look at the immediate context for some indication of what the word might mean. Contextual clues can often give you all the information you need to decipher the meaning of an unfamiliar word. Even if you can't determine the meaning, you may be able to narrow down the possibilities enough to make a solid guess at the answer to the question.

⊘ PREFIXES

If you're having trouble with a word in the question or answer choices, try dissecting it. Take advantage of every clue that the word might include. Prefixes can be a huge help. Usually, they allow you to determine a basic meaning. *Pre-* means before, *post-* means after, *pro-* is positive, *de-* is negative. From prefixes, you can get an idea of the general meaning of the word and try to put it into context.

⊘ HEDGE WORDS

Watch out for critical hedge words, such as *likely, may, can, sometimes, often, almost, mostly, usually, generally, rarely,* and *sometimes.* Question writers insert these hedge phrases to cover every possibility. Often an answer choice will be wrong simply because it leaves no room for exception. Be on guard for answer choices that have definitive words such as *exactly* and *always.*

⊘ SWITCHBACK WORDS

Stay alert for *switchbacks.* These are the words and phrases frequently used to alert you to shifts in thought. The most common switchback words are *but, although,* and *however.* Others include *nevertheless, on the other hand, even though, while, in spite of, despite,* and *regardless of.* Switchback words are important to catch because they can change the direction of the question or an answer choice.

☑ FACE VALUE

When in doubt, use common sense. Accept the situation in the problem at face value. Don't read too much into it. These problems will not require you to make wild assumptions. If you have to go beyond creativity and warp time or space in order to have an answer choice fit the question, then you should move on and consider the other answer choices. These are normal problems rooted in reality. The applicable relationship or explanation may not be readily apparent, but it is there for you to figure out. Use your common sense to interpret anything that isn't clear.

Answer Choice Strategies

☑ ANSWER SELECTION

The most thorough way to pick an answer choice is to identify and eliminate wrong answers until only one is left, then confirm it is the correct answer. Sometimes an answer choice may immediately seem right, but be careful. The test writers will usually put more than one reasonable answer choice on each question, so take a second to read all of them and make sure that the other choices are not equally obvious. As long as you have time left, it is better to read every answer choice than to pick the first one that looks right without checking the others.

☑ ANSWER CHOICE FAMILIES

An answer choice family consists of two (in rare cases, three) answer choices that are very similar in construction and cannot all be true at the same time. If you see two answer choices that are direct opposites or parallels, one of them is usually the correct answer. For instance, if one answer choice says that quantity x increases and another either says that quantity x decreases (opposite) or says that quantity y increases (parallel), then those answer choices would fall into the same family. An answer choice that doesn't match the construction of the answer choice family is more likely to be incorrect. Most questions will not have answer choice families, but when they do appear, you should be prepared to recognize them.

☑ ELIMINATE ANSWERS

Eliminate answer choices as soon as you realize they are wrong, but make sure you consider all possibilities. If you are eliminating answer choices and realize that the last one you are left with is also wrong, don't panic. Start over and consider each choice again. There may be something you missed the first time that you will realize on the second pass.

☑ AVOID FACT TRAPS

Don't be distracted by an answer choice that is factually true but doesn't answer the question. You are looking for the choice that answers the question. Stay focused on what the question is asking for so you don't accidentally pick an answer that is true but incorrect. Always go back to the question and make sure the answer choice you've selected actually answers the question and is not merely a true statement.

☑ EXTREME STATEMENTS

In general, you should avoid answers that put forth extreme actions as standard practice or proclaim controversial ideas as established fact. An answer choice that states the "process should be used in certain situations, if…" is much more likely to be correct than one that states the "process should be discontinued completely." The first is a calm rational statement and doesn't even make a definitive, uncompromising stance, using a hedge word *if* to provide wiggle room, whereas the second choice is far more extreme.

⊘ Benchmark

As you read through the answer choices and you come across one that seems to answer the question well, mentally select that answer choice. This is not your final answer, but it's the one that will help you evaluate the other answer choices. The one that you selected is your benchmark or standard for judging each of the other answer choices. Every other answer choice must be compared to your benchmark. That choice is correct until proven otherwise by another answer choice beating it. If you find a better answer, then that one becomes your new benchmark. Once you've decided that no other choice answers the question as well as your benchmark, you have your final answer.

⊘ Predict the Answer

Before you even start looking at the answer choices, it is often best to try to predict the answer. When you come up with the answer on your own, it is easier to avoid distractions and traps because you will know exactly what to look for. The right answer choice is unlikely to be word-for-word what you came up with, but it should be a close match. Even if you are confident that you have the right answer, you should still take the time to read each option before moving on.

General Strategies

⊘ Tough Questions

If you are stumped on a problem or it appears too hard or too difficult, don't waste time. Move on! Remember though, if you can quickly check for obviously incorrect answer choices, your chances of guessing correctly are greatly improved. Before you completely give up, at least try to knock out a couple of possible answers. Eliminate what you can and then guess at the remaining answer choices before moving on.

⊘ Check Your Work

Since you will probably not know every term listed and the answer to every question, it is important that you get credit for the ones that you do know. Don't miss any questions through careless mistakes. If at all possible, try to take a second to look back over your answer selection and make sure you've selected the correct answer choice and haven't made a costly careless mistake (such as marking an answer choice that you didn't mean to mark). This quick double check should more than pay for itself in caught mistakes for the time it costs.

⊘ Pace Yourself

It's easy to be overwhelmed when you're looking at a page full of questions; your mind is confused and full of random thoughts, and the clock is ticking down faster than you would like. Calm down and maintain the pace that you have set for yourself. Especially as you get down to the last few minutes of the test, don't let the small numbers on the clock make you panic. As long as you are on track by monitoring your pace, you are guaranteed to have time for each question.

⊘ Don't Rush

It is very easy to make errors when you are in a hurry. Maintaining a fast pace in answering questions is pointless if it makes you miss questions that you would have gotten right otherwise. Test writers like to include distracting information and wrong answers that seem right. Taking a little extra time to avoid careless mistakes can make all the difference in your test score. Find a pace that allows you to be confident in the answers that you select.

9

⊘ KEEP MOVING

Panicking will not help you pass the test, so do your best to stay calm and keep moving. Taking deep breaths and going through the answer elimination steps you practiced can help to break through a stress barrier and keep your pace.

Final Notes

The combination of a solid foundation of content knowledge and the confidence that comes from practicing your plan for applying that knowledge is the key to maximizing your performance on test day. As your foundation of content knowledge is built up and strengthened, you'll find that the strategies included in this chapter become more and more effective in helping you quickly sift through the distractions and traps of the test to isolate the correct answer.

Now that you're preparing to move forward into the test content chapters of this book, be sure to keep your goal in mind. As you read, think about how you will be able to apply this information on the test. If you've already seen sample questions for the test and you have an idea of the question format and style, try to come up with questions of your own that you can answer based on what you're reading. This will give you valuable practice applying your knowledge in the same ways you can expect to on test day.

Good luck and good studying!

Operations with Real Numbers and Expressions

Number Basics

CLASSIFICATIONS OF NUMBERS

Numbers are the basic building blocks of mathematics. Specific features of numbers are identified by the following terms:

Integer – any positive or negative whole number, including zero. Integers do not include fractions $\left(\frac{1}{3}\right)$, decimals (0.56), or mixed numbers $\left(7\frac{3}{4}\right)$.

Prime number – any whole number greater than 1 that has only two factors, itself and 1; that is, a number that can be divided evenly only by 1 and itself.

Composite number – any whole number greater than 1 that has more than two different factors; in other words, any whole number that is not a prime number. For example: The composite number 8 has the factors of 1, 2, 4, and 8.

Even number – any integer that can be divided by 2 without leaving a remainder. For example: 2, 4, 6, 8, and so on.

Odd number – any integer that cannot be divided evenly by 2. For example: 3, 5, 7, 9, and so on.

Decimal number – any number that uses a decimal point to show the part of the number that is less than one. Example: 1.234.

Decimal point – a symbol used to separate the ones place from the tenths place in decimals or dollars from cents in currency.

Decimal place – the position of a number to the right of the decimal point. In the decimal 0.123, the 1 is in the first place to the right of the decimal point, indicating tenths; the 2 is in the second place, indicating hundredths; and the 3 is in the third place, indicating thousandths.

The **decimal**, or base 10, system is a number system that uses ten different digits (0, 1, 2, 3, 4, 5, 6, 7, 8, 9). An example of a number system that uses something other than ten digits is the **binary**, or base 2, number system, used by computers, which uses only the numbers 0 and 1. It is thought that the decimal system originated because people had only their 10 fingers for counting.

Rational numbers include all integers, decimals, and fractions. Any terminating or repeating decimal number is a rational number.

Irrational numbers cannot be written as fractions or decimals because the number of decimal places is infinite and there is no recurring pattern of digits within the number. For example, pi (π) begins with 3.141592 and continues without terminating or repeating, so pi is an irrational number.

11

Real numbers are the set of all rational and irrational numbers.

NUMBERS IN WORD FORM AND PLACE VALUE

When writing numbers out in word form or translating word form to numbers, it is essential to understand how a place value system works. In the decimal or base-10 system, each digit of a number represents how many of the corresponding place value—a specific factor of 10—are contained in the number being represented. To make reading numbers easier, every three digits to the left of the decimal place is preceded by a comma. The following table demonstrates some of the place values:

Power of 10	10^3	10^2	10^1	10^0	10^{-1}	10^{-2}	10^{-3}
Value	1,000	100	10	1	0.1	0.01	0.001
Place	thousands	hundreds	tens	ones	tenths	hundredths	thousandths

For example, consider the number 4,546.09, which can be separated into each place value like this:

4: thousands
5: hundreds
4: tens
6: ones
0: tenths
9: hundredths

This number in word form would be *four thousand five hundred forty-six and nine hundredths.*

Rational Numbers

The term **rational** means that the number can be expressed as a ratio or fraction. That is, a number, r, is rational if and only if it can be represented by a fraction $\frac{a}{b}$ where a and b are integers and b does not equal 0. The set of rational numbers includes integers and decimals. If there is no finite way to represent a value with a fraction of integers, then the number is **irrational**. Common examples of irrational numbers include: $\sqrt{5}$, $\left(1 + \sqrt{2}\right)$, and π.

Number Lines

A number line is a graph to see the distance between numbers. Basically, this graph shows the relationship between numbers. So a number line may have a point for zero and may show negative numbers on the left side of the line. Any positive numbers are placed on the right side of the line. For example, consider the points labeled on the following number line:

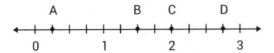

We can use the dashed lines on the number line to identify each point. Each dashed line between two whole numbers is $\frac{1}{4}$. The line halfway between two numbers is $\frac{1}{2}$.

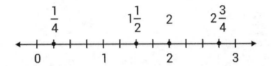

Review Video: **The Number Line**
Visit mometrix.com/academy and enter code: 816439

Absolute Value

A precursor to working with negative numbers is understanding what **absolute values** are. A number's absolute value is simply the distance away from zero a number is on the number line. The absolute value of a number is always positive and is written $|x|$. For example, the absolute value of 3, written as $|3|$, is 3 because the distance between 0 and 3 on a number line is three units. Likewise, the absolute value of –3, written as $|-3|$, is 3 because the distance between 0 and –3 on a number line is three units. So $|3| = |-3|$.

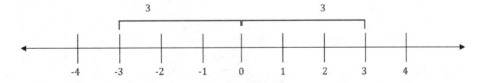

Review Video: **Absolute Value**
Visit mometrix.com/academy and enter code: 314669

Operations

An **operation** is simply a mathematical process that takes some value(s) as input(s) and produces an output. Elementary operations are often written in the following form: *value operation value*. For instance, in the expression $1 + 2$ the values are 1 and 2 and the operation is addition. Performing the operation gives the output of 3. In this way we can say that $1 + 2$ and 3 are equal, or $1 + 2 = 3$.

ADDITION

Addition increases the value of one quantity by the value of another quantity (both called **addends**). Example: $2 + 4 = 6$ or $8 + 9 = 17$. The result is called the **sum**. With addition, the order does not matter, $4 + 2 = 2 + 4$.

When adding signed numbers, if the signs are the same simply add the absolute values of the addends and apply the original sign to the sum. For example, $(+4) + (+8) = +12$ and $(-4) + (-8) = -12$. When the original signs are different, take the absolute values of the addends and subtract the smaller value from the larger value, then apply the original sign of the larger value to the difference. Example: $(+4) + (-8) = -4$ and $(-4) + (+8) = +4$.

SUBTRACTION

Subtraction is the opposite operation to addition; it decreases the value of one quantity (the **minuend**) by the value of another quantity (the **subtrahend**). For example, $6 - 4 = 2$ or $17 - 8 = 9$. The result is called the **difference**. Note that with subtraction, the order does matter, $6 - 4 \neq 4 - 6$.

For subtracting signed numbers, change the sign of the subtrahend and then follow the same rules used for addition. Example: $(+4) - (+8) = (+4) + (-8) = -4$

MULTIPLICATION

Multiplication can be thought of as repeated addition. One number (the **multiplier**) indicates how many times to add the other number (the **multiplicand**) to itself. Example: $3 \times 2 = 2 + 2 + 2 = 6$. With multiplication, the order does not matter, $2 \times 3 = 3 \times 2$ or $3 + 3 = 2 + 2 + 2$, either way the result (the **product**) is the same.

If the signs are the same, the product is positive when multiplying signed numbers. Example: $(+4) \times (+8) = +32$ and $(-4) \times (-8) = +32$. If the signs are opposite, the product is negative. Example: $(+4) \times (-8) = -32$ and $(-4) \times (+8) = -32$. When more than two factors are multiplied together, the sign of the product is determined by how many negative factors are present. If there are an odd number of negative factors then the product is negative, whereas an even number of negative factors indicates a positive product. Example: $(+4) \times (-8) \times (-2) = +64$ and $(-4) \times (-8) \times (-2) = -64$.

DIVISION

Division is the opposite operation to multiplication; one number (the **divisor**) tells us how many parts to divide the other number (the **dividend**) into. The result of division is called the **quotient**. Example: $20 \div 4 = 5$. If 20 is split into 4 equal parts, each part is 5. With division, the order of the numbers does matter, $20 \div 4 \neq 4 \div 20$.

The rules for dividing signed numbers are similar to multiplying signed numbers. If the dividend and divisor have the same sign, the quotient is positive. If the dividend and divisor have opposite signs, the quotient is negative. Example: $(-4) \div (+8) = -0.5$.

> **Review Video: Mathematical Operations**
> Visit mometrix.com/academy and enter code: 208095

PARENTHESES

Parentheses are used to designate which operations should be done first when there are multiple operations. Example: $4 - (2 + 1) = 1$; the parentheses tell us that we must add 2 and 1, and then subtract the sum from 4, rather than subtracting 2 from 4 and then adding 1 (this would give us an answer of 3).

EXPONENTS

An **exponent** is a superscript number placed next to another number at the top right. It indicates how many times the base number is to be multiplied by itself. Exponents provide a shorthand way to write what would be a longer mathematical expression, Example: $2^4 = 2 \times 2 \times 2 \times 2$. A number with an exponent of 2 is said to be "squared," while a number with an exponent of 3 is said to be "cubed." The value of a number raised to an exponent is called its power. So 8^4 is read as "8 to the 4th power," or "8 raised to the power of 4."

ROOTS

A **root**, such as a square root, is another way of writing a fractional exponent. Instead of using a superscript, roots use the radical symbol ($\sqrt{}$) to indicate the operation. A radical will have a number underneath the bar, and may sometimes have a number in the upper left: $\sqrt[n]{a}$, read as "the nth root of a." The relationship between radical notation and exponent notation can be described by this equation:

$$\sqrt[n]{a} = a^{\frac{1}{n}}$$

The two special cases of $n = 2$ and $n = 3$ are called square roots and cube roots. If there is no number to the upper left, the radical is understood to be a square root ($n = 2$). Nearly all of the roots you encounter will be square roots. A square root is the same as a number raised to the one-half power. When we say that a is the square root of b ($a = \sqrt{b}$), we mean that a multiplied by itself equals b: ($a \times a = b$).

A **perfect square** is a number that has an integer for its square root. There are 10 perfect squares from 1 to 100: 1, 4, 9, 16, 25, 36, 49, 64, 81, 100 (the squares of integers 1 through 10).

WORD PROBLEMS AND MATHEMATICAL SYMBOLS

When working on word problems, you must be able to translate verbal expressions or "math words" into math symbols. This chart contains several "math words" and their appropriate symbols:

Phrase	Symbol
equal, is, was, will be, has, costs, gets to, is the same as, becomes	=
times, of, multiplied by, product of, twice, doubles, halves, triples	×
divided by, per, ratio of/to, out of	÷
plus, added to, sum, combined, and, more than, totals of	+
subtracted from, less than, decreased by, minus, difference between	−
what, how much, original value, how many, a number, a variable	x, n, etc.

EXAMPLES OF TRANSLATED MATHEMATICAL PHRASES

- The phrase four more than twice a number can be written algebraically as $2x + 4$.
- The phrase half a number decreased by six can be written algebraically as $\frac{1}{2}x - 6$.
- The phrase the sum of a number and the product of five and that number can be written algebraically as $x + 5x$.
- You may see a test question that says, "Olivia is constructing a bookcase from seven boards. Two of them are for vertical supports and five are for shelves. The height of the bookcase is twice the width of the bookcase. If the seven boards total 36 feet in length, what will be the height of Olivia's bookcase?" You would need to make a sketch and then create the equation to determine the width of the shelves. The height can be represented as double the width. (If x represents the width of the shelves in feet, then the height of the bookcase is $2x$. Since the seven boards total 36 feet, $2x + 2x + x + x + x + x + x = 36$ or $9x = 36$; $x = 4$. The height is twice the width, or 8 feet.)

Subtraction with Regrouping

A great way to make use of some of the features built into the decimal system would be regrouping when attempting longform subtraction operations. When subtracting within a place value, sometimes the minuend is smaller than the subtrahend, **regrouping** enables you to 'borrow' a unit from a place value to the left in order to get a positive difference. For example, consider subtracting 189 from 525 with regrouping.

First, set up the subtraction problem in vertical form:

```
   525
-  189
_____
```

Notice that the numbers in the ones and tens columns of 525 are smaller than the numbers in the ones and tens columns of 189. This means you will need to use regrouping to perform subtraction:

```
   5   2   5
-  1   8   9
_____
```

16

To subtract 9 from 5 in the ones column you will need to borrow from the 2 in the tens columns:

```
      5    1   15
  −   1    8    9
                6
```

Next, to subtract 8 from 1 in the tens column you will need to borrow from the 5 in the hundreds column:

```
      4   11   15
  −   1    8    9
           3    6
```

Last, subtract the 1 from the 4 in the hundreds column:

```
      4   11   15
  −   1    8    9
      3    3    6
```

> **Review Video: Subtracting Large Numbers**
> Visit mometrix.com/academy and enter code: 603350

Order of Operations

The **order of operations** is a set of rules that dictates the order in which we must perform each operation in an expression so that we will evaluate it accurately. If we have an expression that includes multiple different operations, the order of operations tells us which operations to do first. The most common mnemonic for the order of operations is **PEMDAS**, or "Please Excuse My Dear Aunt Sally." PEMDAS stands for parentheses, exponents, multiplication, division, addition, and subtraction. It is important to understand that multiplication and division have equal precedence, as do addition and subtraction, so those pairs of operations are simply worked from left to right in order.

For example, evaluating the expression $5 + 20 \div 4 \times (2 + 3)^2 − 6$ using the correct order of operations would be done like this:

- **P:** Perform the operations inside the parentheses: $(2 + 3) = 5$
- **E:** Simplify the exponents: $(5)^2 = 5 \times 5 = 25$
  - o   The expression now looks like this: $5 + 20 \div 4 \times 25 − 6$
- **MD:** Perform multiplication and division from left to right: $20 \div 4 = 5$; then $5 \times 25 = 125$
  - o   The expression now looks like this: $5 + 125 − 6$
- **AS:** Perform addition and subtraction from left to right: $5 + 125 = 130$; then $130 − 6 = 124$

> **Review Video: Order of Operations**
> Visit mometrix.com/academy and enter code: 259675

Properties of Exponents

The properties of exponents are as follows:

Property	Description
$a^1 = a$	Any number to the power of 1 is equal to itself
$1^n = 1$	The number 1 raised to any power is equal to 1
$a^0 = 1$	Any number raised to the power of 0 is equal to 1
$a^n \times a^m = a^{n+m}$	Add exponents to multiply powers of the same base number
$a^n \div a^m = a^{n-m}$	Subtract exponents to divide powers of the same base number
$(a^n)^m = a^{n \times m}$	When a power is raised to a power, the exponents are multiplied
$(a \times b)^n = a^n \times b^n$ $(a \div b)^n = a^n \div b^n$	Multiplication and division operations inside parentheses can be raised to a power. This is the same as each term being raised to that power.
$a^{-n} = \dfrac{1}{a^n}$	A negative exponent is the same as the reciprocal of a positive exponent

Note that exponents do not have to be integers. Fractional or decimal exponents follow all the rules above as well. Example: $5^{\frac{1}{4}} \times 5^{\frac{3}{4}} = 5^{\frac{1}{4}+\frac{3}{4}} = 5^1 = 5$.

> **Review Video: Properties of Exponents**
> Visit mometrix.com/academy and enter code: 532558

Factors and Multiples

FACTORS AND GREATEST COMMON FACTOR

Factors are numbers that are multiplied together to obtain a **product**. For example, in the equation $2 \times 3 = 6$, the numbers 2 and 3 are factors. A **prime number** has only two factors (1 and itself), but other numbers can have many factors.

A **common factor** is a number that divides exactly into two or more other numbers. For example, the factors of 12 are 1, 2, 3, 4, 6, and 12, while the factors of 15 are 1, 3, 5, and 15. The common factors of 12 and 15 are 1 and 3.

A **prime factor** is also a prime number. Therefore, the prime factors of 12 are 2 and 3. For 15, the prime factors are 3 and 5.

The **greatest common factor** (GCF) is the largest number that is a factor of two or more numbers. For example, the factors of 15 are 1, 3, 5, and 15; the factors of 35 are 1, 5, 7, and 35. Therefore, the greatest common factor of 15 and 35 is 5.

> **Review Video: Factors**
> Visit mometrix.com/academy and enter code: 920086
>
> **Review Video: Prime Numbers and Factorization**
> Visit mometrix.com/academy and enter code: 760669

MULTIPLES AND LEAST COMMON MULTIPLE

Often listed out in multiplication tables, **multiples** are integer increments of a given factor. In other words, dividing a multiple by the factor will result in an integer. For example, the multiples of 7 include: $1 \times 7 = 7, 2 \times 7 = 14, 3 \times 7 = 21, 4 \times 7 = 28, 5 \times 7 = 35$. Dividing 7, 14, 21, 28, or 35 by 7 will result in the integers 1, 2, 3, 4, and 5, respectively.

The least common multiple (**LCM**) is the smallest number that is a multiple of two or more numbers. For example, the multiples of 3 include 3, 6, 9, 12, 15, etc.; the multiples of 5 include 5, 10, 15, 20, etc. Therefore, the least common multiple of 3 and 5 is 15.

Fractions, Decimals, and Percentages

FRACTIONS

A **fraction** is a number that is expressed as one integer written above another integer, with a dividing line between them $\left(\frac{x}{y}\right)$. It represents the **quotient** of the two numbers "x divided by y." It can also be thought of as x out of y equal parts.

The top number of a fraction is called the **numerator**, and it represents the number of parts under consideration. The 1 in $\frac{1}{4}$ means that 1 part out of the whole is being considered in the calculation. The bottom number of a fraction is called the **denominator**, and it represents the total number of equal parts. The 4 in $\frac{1}{4}$ means that the whole consists of 4 equal parts. A fraction cannot have a denominator of zero; this is referred to as "*undefined*."

Fractions can be manipulated, without changing the value of the fraction, by multiplying or dividing (but not adding or subtracting) both the numerator and denominator by the same number. If you divide both numbers by a common factor, you are **reducing** or simplifying the fraction. Two fractions that have the same value but are expressed differently are known as **equivalent fractions**. For example, $\frac{2}{10}, \frac{3}{15}, \frac{4}{20}$, and $\frac{5}{25}$ are all equivalent fractions. They can also all be reduced or simplified to $\frac{1}{5}$.

When two fractions are manipulated so that they have the same denominator, this is known as finding a **common denominator**. The number chosen to be that common denominator should be the least common multiple of the two original denominators. Example: $\frac{3}{4}$ and $\frac{5}{6}$; the least common multiple of 4 and 6 is 12. Manipulating to achieve the common denominator: $\frac{3}{4} = \frac{9}{12}; \frac{5}{6} = \frac{10}{12}$.

PROPER FRACTIONS AND MIXED NUMBERS

A fraction whose denominator is greater than its numerator is known as a **proper fraction**, while a fraction whose numerator is greater than its denominator is known as an **improper fraction**. Proper fractions have values *less than one* and improper fractions have values *greater than one*.

A **mixed number** is a number that contains both an integer and a fraction. Any improper fraction can be rewritten as a mixed number. Example: $\frac{8}{3} = \frac{6}{3} + \frac{2}{3} = 2 + \frac{2}{3} = 2\frac{2}{3}$. Similarly, any mixed number can be rewritten as an improper fraction. Example: $1\frac{3}{5} = 1 + \frac{3}{5} = \frac{5}{5} + \frac{3}{5} = \frac{8}{5}$.

ADDING AND SUBTRACTING FRACTIONS

If two fractions have a common denominator, they can be added or subtracted simply by adding or subtracting the two numerators and retaining the same denominator. If the two fractions do not already have the same denominator, one or both of them must be manipulated to achieve a common denominator before they can be added or subtracted. Example: $\frac{1}{2} + \frac{1}{4} = \frac{2}{4} + \frac{1}{4} = \frac{3}{4}$.

MULTIPLYING FRACTIONS

Two fractions can be multiplied by multiplying the two numerators to find the new numerator and the two denominators to find the new denominator. Example: $\frac{1}{3} \times \frac{2}{3} = \frac{1 \times 2}{3 \times 3} = \frac{2}{9}$.

DIVIDING FRACTIONS

Two fractions can be divided by flipping the numerator and denominator of the second fraction and then proceeding as though it were a multiplication problem. Example: $\frac{2}{3} \div \frac{3}{4} = \frac{2}{3} \times \frac{4}{3} = \frac{8}{9}$.

MULTIPLYING A MIXED NUMBER BY A WHOLE NUMBER OR A DECIMAL

When multiplying a mixed number by something, it is usually best to convert it to an improper fraction first. Additionally, if the multiplicand is a decimal, it is most often simplest to convert it to a fraction. For instance, to multiply $4\frac{3}{8}$ by 3.5, begin by rewriting each quantity as a whole number plus a proper fraction. Remember, a mixed number is a fraction added to a whole number and a decimal is a representation of the sum of fractions, specifically tenths, hundredths, thousandths, and so on:

$$4\frac{3}{8} \times 3.5 = \left(4 + \frac{3}{8}\right) \times \left(3 + \frac{1}{2}\right)$$

Next, the quantities being added need to be expressed with the same denominator. This is achieved by multiplying and dividing the whole number by the denominator of the fraction. Recall that a whole number is equivalent to that number divided by 1:

$$= \left(\frac{4}{1} \times \frac{8}{8} + \frac{3}{8}\right) \times \left(\frac{3}{1} \times \frac{2}{2} + \frac{1}{2}\right)$$

When multiplying fractions, remember to multiply the numerators and denominators separately:

$$= \left(\frac{4 \times 8}{1 \times 8} + \frac{3}{8}\right) \times \left(\frac{3 \times 2}{1 \times 2} + \frac{1}{2}\right)$$

$$= \left(\frac{32}{8} + \frac{3}{8}\right) \times \left(\frac{6}{2} + \frac{1}{2}\right)$$

Now that the fractions have the same denominators, they can be added:

$$= \frac{35}{8} \times \frac{7}{2}$$

Finally, perform the last multiplication and then simplify:

$$= \frac{35 \times 7}{8 \times 2} = \frac{245}{16} = \frac{240}{16} + \frac{5}{16} = 15\frac{5}{16}$$

COMPARING FRACTIONS

It is important to master the ability to compare and order fractions. This skill is relevant to many real-world scenarios. For example, carpenters often compare fractional construction nail lengths when preparing for a project, and bakers often compare fractional measurements to have the correct ratio of ingredients. There are three commonly used strategies when comparing fractions. These strategies are referred to as the common denominator approach, the decimal approach, and the cross-multiplication approach.

USING A COMMON DENOMINATOR TO COMPARE FRACTIONS

The fractions $\frac{2}{3}$ and $\frac{4}{7}$ have different denominators. $\frac{2}{3}$ has a denominator of 3, and $\frac{4}{7}$ has a denominator of 7. In order to precisely compare these two fractions, it is necessary to use a common denominator. A common denominator is a common multiple that is shared by both denominators. In this case, the denominators 3 and 7 share a multiple of 21. In general, it is most efficient to select the least common multiple for the two denominators.

Rewrite each fraction with the common denominator of 21. Then, calculate the new numerators as illustrated below.

For $\frac{2}{3}$, multiply the numerator and denominator by 7. The result is $\frac{14}{21}$.

For $\frac{4}{7}$, multiply the numerator and denominator by 3. The result is $\frac{12}{21}$.

Now that both fractions have a denominator of 21, the fractions can accurately be compared by comparing the numerators. Since 14 is greater than 12, the fraction $\frac{14}{21}$ is greater than $\frac{12}{21}$. This means that $\frac{2}{3}$ is greater than $\frac{4}{7}$.

USING DECIMALS TO COMPARE FRACTIONS

Sometimes decimal values are easier to compare than fraction values. For example, $\frac{5}{8}$ is equivalent to 0.625 and $\frac{3}{5}$ is equivalent to 0.6. This means that the comparison of $\frac{5}{8}$ and $\frac{3}{5}$ can be determined by comparing the decimals 0.625 and 0.6. When both decimal values are extended to the thousandths place, they become 0.625 and 0.600, respectively. It becomes clear that 0.625 is greater than 0.600 because 625 thousandths is greater than 600 thousandths. In other words, $\frac{5}{8}$ is greater than $\frac{3}{5}$ because 0.625 is greater than 0.6.

USING CROSS-MULTIPLICATION TO COMPARE FRACTIONS

Cross-multiplication is an efficient strategy for comparing fractions. This is a shortcut for the common denominator strategy. Start by writing each fraction next to one another. Multiply the numerator of the fraction on the left by the denominator of the fraction on the right. Write down the result next to the fraction on the left. Now multiply the numerator of the fraction on the right by the denominator of the fraction on the left. Write down the result next to the fraction on the right. Compare both products. The fraction with the larger result is the larger fraction.

Consider the fractions $\frac{4}{7}$ and $\frac{5}{9}$.

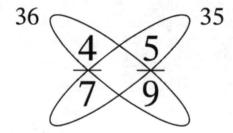

36 is greater than 35. Therefore, $\frac{4}{7}$ is greater than $\frac{5}{9}$.

DECIMALS

Decimals are one way to represent parts of a whole. Using the place value system, each digit to the right of a decimal point denotes the number of units of a corresponding *negative* power of ten. For example, consider the decimal 0.24. We can use a model to represent the decimal. Since a dime is worth one-tenth of a dollar and a penny is worth one-hundredth of a dollar, one possible model to represent this fraction is to have 2 dimes representing the 2 in the tenths place and 4 pennies representing the 4 in the hundredths place:

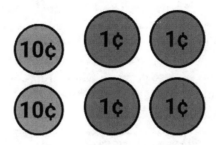

To write the decimal as a fraction, put the decimal in the numerator with 1 in the denominator. Multiply the numerator and denominator by tens until there are no more decimal places. Then simplify the fraction to lowest terms. For example, converting 0.24 to a fraction:

$$0.24 = \frac{0.24}{1} = \frac{0.24 \times 100}{1 \times 100} = \frac{24}{100} = \frac{6}{25}$$

Review Video: Decimals
Visit mometrix.com/academy and enter code: 837268

OPERATIONS WITH DECIMALS
ADDING AND SUBTRACTING DECIMALS

When adding and subtracting decimals, the decimal points must always be aligned. Adding decimals is just like adding regular whole numbers. Example: $4.5 + 2.0 = 6.5$.

If the problem-solver does not properly align the decimal points, an incorrect answer of 4.7 may result. An easy way to add decimals is to align all of the decimal points in a vertical column visually. This will allow you to see exactly where the decimal should be placed in the final answer. Begin adding from right to left. Add each column in turn, making sure to carry the number to the left if a column adds up to more than 9. The same rules apply to the subtraction of decimals.

Review Video: Adding and Subtracting Decimals
Visit mometrix.com/academy and enter code: 381101

MULTIPLYING DECIMALS

A simple multiplication problem has two components: a **multiplicand** and a **multiplier**. When multiplying decimals, work as though the numbers were whole rather than decimals. Once the final product is calculated, count the number of places to the right of the decimal in both the multiplicand and the multiplier. Then, count that number of places from the right of the product and place the decimal in that position.

For example, 12.3×2.56 has a total of three places to the right of the respective decimals. Multiply 123×256 to get 31,488. Now, beginning on the right, count three places to the left and insert the decimal. The final product will be 31.488.

Review Video: How to Multiply Decimals
Visit mometrix.com/academy and enter code: 731574

DIVIDING DECIMALS

Every division problem has a **divisor** and a **dividend**. The dividend is the number that is being divided. In the problem $14 \div 7$, 14 is the dividend and 7 is the divisor. In a division problem with decimals, the divisor must be converted into a whole number. Begin by moving the decimal in the divisor to the right until a whole number is created. Next, move the decimal in the dividend the same number of spaces to the right. For example, 4.9 into 24.5 would become 49 into 245. The decimal was moved one space to the right to create a whole number in the divisor, and then the same was done for the dividend. Once the whole numbers are created, the problem is carried out normally: $245 \div 49 = 5$.

> **Review Video: <u>Dividing Decimals</u>**
> Visit mometrix.com/academy and enter code: 560690
>
> **Review Video: <u>Dividing Decimals by Whole Numbers</u>**
> Visit mometrix.com/academy and enter code: 535669

PERCENTAGES

Percentages can be thought of as fractions that are based on a whole of 100; that is, one whole is equal to 100%. The word **percent** means "per hundred." Percentage problems are often presented in three main ways:

- Find what percentage of some number another number is.
  - Example: What percentage of 40 is 8?
- Find what number is some percentage of a given number.
  - Example: What number is 20% of 40?
- Find what number another number is a given percentage of.
  - Example: What number is 8 20% of?

There are three components in each of these cases: a **whole** (W), a **part** (P), and a **percentage** (%). These are related by the equation: $P = W \times \%$. This can easily be rearranged into other forms that may suit different questions better: $\% = \frac{P}{W}$ and $W = \frac{P}{\%}$. Percentage problems are often also word problems. As such, a large part of solving them is figuring out which quantities are what. For example, consider the following word problem:

In a school cafeteria, 7 students choose pizza, 9 choose hamburgers, and 4 choose tacos. What percentage of student choose tacos?

To find the whole, you must first add all of the parts: $7 + 9 + 4 = 20$. The percentage can then be found by dividing the part by the whole $\left(\% = \frac{P}{W}\right) : \frac{4}{20} = \frac{20}{100} = 20\%$.

> **Review Video: <u>Computation with Percentages</u>**
> Visit mometrix.com/academy and enter code: 693099

CONVERTING BETWEEN PERCENTAGES, FRACTIONS, AND DECIMALS

Converting decimals to percentages and percentages to decimals is as simple as moving the decimal point. To *convert from a decimal to a percentage*, move the decimal point **two places to the right**. To *convert from a percentage to a decimal*, move it **two places to the left**. It may be helpful to remember that the percentage number will always be larger than the equivalent decimal number. Example:

$$0.23 = 23\% \quad 5.34 = 534\% \quad 0.007 = 0.7\%$$
$$700\% = 7.00 \quad 86\% = 0.86 \quad 0.15\% = 0.0015$$

To convert a fraction to a decimal, simply divide the numerator by the denominator in the fraction. To convert a decimal to a fraction, put the decimal in the numerator with 1 in the denominator. Multiply the numerator and denominator by tens until there are no more decimal places. Then simplify the fraction to lowest terms. For example, converting 0.24 to a fraction:

$$0.24 = \frac{0.24}{1} = \frac{0.24 \times 100}{1 \times 100} = \frac{24}{100} = \frac{6}{25}$$

Fractions can be converted to a percentage by finding equivalent fractions with a denominator of 100. Example:

$$\frac{7}{10} = \frac{70}{100} = 70\% \quad \frac{1}{4} = \frac{25}{100} = 25\%$$

To convert a percentage to a fraction, divide the percentage number by 100 and reduce the fraction to its simplest possible terms. Example:

$$60\% = \frac{60}{100} = \frac{3}{5} \quad 96\% = \frac{96}{100} = \frac{24}{25}$$

> **Review Video: <u>Converting Fractions to Percentages and Decimals</u>**
> Visit mometrix.com/academy and enter code: 306233
>
> **Review Video: <u>Converting Percentages to Decimals and Fractions</u>**
> Visit mometrix.com/academy and enter code: 287297
>
> **Review Video: <u>Converting Decimals to Fractions and Percentages</u>**
> Visit mometrix.com/academy and enter code: 986765
>
> **Review Video: <u>Converting Decimals, Improper Fractions, and Mixed Numbers</u>**
> Visit mometrix.com/academy and enter code: 696924

Proportions and Ratios

PROPORTIONS

A proportion is a relationship between two quantities that dictates how one changes when the other changes. A **direct proportion** describes a relationship in which a quantity increases by a set amount for every increase in the other quantity, or decreases by that same amount for every decrease in the other quantity. Example: Assuming a constant driving speed, the time required for a car trip increases as the distance of the trip increases. The distance to be traveled and the time required to travel are directly proportional.

An **inverse proportion** is a relationship in which an increase in one quantity is accompanied by a decrease in the other, or vice versa. Example: the time required for a car trip decreases as the speed increases and increases as the speed decreases, so the time required is inversely proportional to the speed of the car.

Review Video: <u>Proportions</u>
Visit mometrix.com/academy and enter code: 505355

RATIOS

A **ratio** is a comparison of two quantities in a particular order. Example: If there are 14 computers in a lab, and the class has 20 students, there is a student to computer ratio of 20 to 14, commonly written as 20: 14. Ratios are normally reduced to their smallest whole number representation, so 20: 14 would be reduced to 10: 7 by dividing both sides by 2.

Review Video: <u>Ratios</u>
Visit mometrix.com/academy and enter code: 996914

CONSTANT OF PROPORTIONALITY

When two quantities have a proportional relationship, there exists a **constant of proportionality** between the quantities. The product of this constant and one of the quantities is equal to the other quantity. For example, if one lemon costs \$0.25, two lemons cost \$0.50, and three lemons cost \$0.75, there is a proportional relationship between the total cost of lemons and the number of lemons purchased. The constant of proportionality is the **unit price**, namely \$0.25/lemon. Notice that the total price of lemons, t, can be found by multiplying the unit price of lemons, p, and the number of lemons, n: $t = pn$.

WORK/UNIT RATE

Unit rate expresses a quantity of one thing in terms of one unit of another. For example, if you travel 30 miles every two hours, a unit rate expresses this comparison in terms of one hour: in one hour you travel 15 miles, so your unit rate is 15 miles per hour. Other examples are how much one ounce of food costs (price per ounce) or figuring out how much one egg costs out of the dozen (price per 1 egg, instead of price per 12 eggs). The denominator of a unit rate is always 1. Unit rates are used to compare different situations to solve problems. For example, to make sure you get the best deal when deciding which kind of soda to buy, you can find the unit rate of each. If soda #1 costs \$1.50 for a 1-liter bottle, and soda #2 costs \$2.75 for a 2-liter bottle, it would be a better deal to buy soda #2, because its unit rate is only \$1.375 per 1-liter, which is cheaper than soda #1. Unit rates can also help determine the length of time a given event will take. For example, if you can paint 2 rooms in 4.5 hours, you can determine how long it will take you to paint 5 rooms by solving for the unit rate per room and then multiplying that by 5.

Review Video: <u>Rates and Unit Rates</u>
Visit mometrix.com/academy and enter code: 185363

Slope

On a graph with two points, (x_1, y_1) and (x_2, y_2), the **slope** is found with the formula $m = \frac{y_2 - y_1}{x_2 - x_1}$; where $x_1 \neq x_2$ and m stands for slope. If the value of the slope is **positive**, the line has an *upward direction* from left to right. If the value of the slope is **negative**, the line has a *downward direction* from left to right. Consider the following example:

A new book goes on sale in bookstores and online stores. In the first month, 5,000 copies of the book are sold. Over time, the book continues to grow in popularity. The data for the number of copies sold is in the table below.

# of Months on Sale	1	2	3	4	5
# of Copies Sold (In Thousands)	5	10	15	20	25

So, the number of copies that are sold and the time that the book is on sale is a proportional relationship. In this example, an equation can be used to show the data: $y = 5x$, where x is the number of months that the book is on sale. Also, y is the number of copies sold. So, the slope of the corresponding line is $\frac{\text{rise}}{\text{run}} = \frac{5}{1} = 5$.

> **Review Video: <u>Finding the Slope of a Line</u>**
> Visit mometrix.com/academy and enter code: 766664

Cross Multiplication

FINDING AN UNKNOWN IN EQUIVALENT EXPRESSIONS

It is often necessary to apply information given about a rate or proportion to a new scenario. For example, if you know that Jedha can run a marathon (26.2 miles) in 3 hours, how long would it take her to run 10 miles at the same pace? Start by setting up equivalent expressions:

$$\frac{26.2 \text{ mi}}{3 \text{ hr}} = \frac{10 \text{ mi}}{x \text{ hr}}$$

Now, cross multiply and solve for x:

$$26.2x = 30$$
$$x = \frac{30}{26.2} = \frac{15}{13.1}$$
$$x \approx 1.15 \text{ hrs } or \text{ 1 hr 9 min}$$

So, at this pace, Jedha could run 10 miles in about 1.15 hours or about 1 hour and 9 minutes.

> **Review Video: <u>Cross Multiplying Fractions</u>**
> Visit mometrix.com/academy and enter code: 893904

Operations and Linear Equations and Inequalities

Linear Expressions

TERMS AND COEFFICIENTS

Mathematical expressions consist of a combination of one or more values arranged in terms that are added together. As such, an expression could be just a single number, including zero. A **variable term** is the product of a real number, also called a **coefficient**, and one or more variables, each of which may be raised to an exponent. Expressions may also include numbers without a variable, called **constants** or **constant terms**. The expression $6s^2$, for example, is a single term where the coefficient is the real number 6 and the variable term is s^2. Note that if a term is written as simply a variable to some exponent, like t^2, then the coefficient is 1, because $t^2 = 1t^2$.

LINEAR EXPRESSIONS

A **single variable linear expression** is the sum of a single variable term, where the variable has no exponent, and a constant, which may be zero. For instance, the expression $2w + 7$ has $2w$ as the variable term and 7 as the constant term. It is important to realize that terms are separated by addition or subtraction. Since an expression is a sum of terms, expressions such as $5x - 3$ can be written as $5x + (-3)$ to emphasize that the constant term is negative. A real-world example of a single variable linear expression is the perimeter of a square, four times the side length, often expressed: $4s$.

In general, a **linear expression** is the sum of any number of variable terms so long as none of the variables have an exponent. For example, $3m + 8n - \frac{1}{4}p + 5.5q - 1$ is a linear expression, but $3y^3$ is not. In the same way, the expression for the perimeter of a general triangle, the sum of the side lengths $(a + b + c)$ is considered to be linear, but the expression for the area of a square, the side length squared $(s^2)$is not.

Linear Equations

Equations that can be written as $ax + b = 0$, where $a \neq 0$, are referred to as **one variable linear equations**. A solution to such an equation is called a **root**. In the case where we have the equation $5x + 10 = 0$, if we solve for x we get a solution of $x = -2$. In other words, the root of the equation is –2. This is found by first subtracting 10 from both sides, which gives $5x = -10$. Next, simply divide both sides by the coefficient of the variable, in this case 5, to get $x = -2$. This can be checked by plugging –2 back into the original equation $(5)(-2) + 10 = -10 + 10 = 0$.

The **solution set** is the set of all solutions of an equation. In our example, the solution set would simply be –2. If there were more solutions (there usually are in multivariable equations) then they would also be included in the solution set. When an equation has no true solutions, it is referred to as an **empty set**. Equations with identical solution sets are **equivalent equations**. An **identity** is a term whose value or determinant is equal to 1.

28

Linear equations can be written many ways. Below is a list of some forms linear equations can take:

- **Standard Form**: $Ax + By = C$; the slope is $\frac{-A}{B}$ and the y-intercept is $\frac{C}{B}$
- **Slope Intercept Form**: $y = mx + b$, where m is the slope and b is the y-intercept
- **Point-Slope Form**: $y - y_1 = m(x - x_1)$, where m is the slope and (x_1, y_1) is a point on the line
- **Two-Point Form**: $\frac{y-y_1}{x-x_1} = \frac{y_2-y_1}{x_2-x_1}$, where (x_1, y_1) and (x_2, y_2) are two points on the given line
- **Intercept Form**: $\frac{x}{x_1} + \frac{y}{y_1} = 1$, where $(x_1, 0)$ is the point at which a line intersects the x-axis, and $(0, y_1)$ is the point at which the same line intersects the y-axis

> **Review Video: <u>Slope-Intercept and Point-Slope Forms</u>**
> Visit mometrix.com/academy and enter code: 113216
>
> **Review Video: <u>Linear Equations Basics</u>**
> Visit mometrix.com/academy and enter code: 793005

Solving Equations

SOLVING ONE-VARIABLE LINEAR EQUATIONS

Multiply all terms by the lowest common denominator to eliminate any fractions. Look for addition or subtraction to undo so you can isolate the variable on one side of the equal sign. Divide both sides by the coefficient of the variable. When you have a value for the variable, substitute this value into the original equation to make sure you have a true equation. Consider the following example:

Kim's savings are represented by the table below. Represent her savings, using an equation.

X (Months)	Y (Total Savings)
2	$1,300
5	$2,050
9	$3,050
11	$3,550
16	$4,800

The table shows a function with a constant rate of change, or slope, of 250. Given the points on the table, the slopes can be calculated as $\frac{(2,050-1300)}{(5-2)}$, $\frac{(3,050-2,050)}{(9-5)}$, $\frac{(3,550-3,050)}{(11-9)}$, and $\frac{(4,800-3,550)}{(16-11)}$, each of which equals 250. Thus, the table shows a constant rate of change, indicating a linear function. The slope-intercept form of a linear equation is written as $y = mx + b$, where m represents the slope and b represents the y-intercept. Substituting the slope into this form gives $y = 250x + b$. Substituting corresponding x- and y-values from any point into this equation will give the y-intercept, or b. Using the point, (2, 1,300), gives $1,300 = 250(2) + b$, which simplifies as $b = 800$. Thus, her savings may be represented by the equation, $y = 250x + 800$.

RULES FOR MANIPULATING EQUATIONS

LIKE TERMS

Like terms are terms in an equation that have the same variable, regardless of whether or not they also have the same coefficient. This includes terms that *lack* a variable; all constants (i.e., numbers without variables) are considered like terms. If the equation involves terms with a variable raised to different powers, the like terms are those that have the variable raised to the same power.

For example, consider the equation $x^2 + 3x + 2 = 2x^2 + x - 7 + 2x$. In this equation, 2 and –7 are like terms; they are both constants. $3x$, x, and $2x$ are like terms, they all include the variable x raised to the first power. x^2 and $2x^2$ are like terms, they both include the variable x, raised to the second power. $2x$ and $2x^2$ are not like terms; although they both involve the variable x, the variable is not raised to the same power in both terms. The fact that they have the same coefficient, 2, is not relevant.

> **Review Video: <u>Rules for Manipulating Equations</u>**
> Visit mometrix.com/academy and enter code: 838871

CARRYING OUT THE SAME OPERATION ON BOTH SIDES OF AN EQUATION

When solving an equation, the general procedure is to carry out a series of operations on both sides of an equation, choosing operations that will tend to simplify the equation when doing so. The reason why the same operation must be carried out on both sides of the equation is because that leaves the meaning of the equation unchanged, and yields a result that is equivalent to the original equation. This would not be the case if we carried out an operation on one side of an equation and not the other. Consider what an equation means: it is a statement that two values or expressions are equal. If we carry out the same operation on both sides of the equation—add 3 to both sides, for example—then the two sides of the equation are changed in the same way, and so remain equal. If we do that to only one side of the equation—add 3 to one side but not the other—then that wouldn't be true; if we change one side of the equation but not the other then the two sides are no longer equal.

ADVANTAGE OF COMBINING LIKE TERMS

Combining like terms refers to adding or subtracting like terms—terms with the same variable—and therefore reducing sets of like terms to a single term. The main advantage of doing this is that it simplifies the equation. Often, combining like terms can be done as the first step in solving an equation, though it can also be done later, such as after distributing terms in a product.

For example, consider the equation $2(x + 3) + 3(2 + x + 3) = -4$. The 2 and the 3 in the second set of parentheses are like terms, and we can combine them, yielding $2(x + 3) + 3(x + 5) = -4$. Now we can carry out the multiplications implied by the parentheses, distributing the outer 2 and 3 accordingly: $2x + 6 + 3x + 15 = -4$. The $2x$ and the $3x$ are like terms, and we can add them together: $5x + 6 + 15 = -4$. Now, the constants 6, 15, and –4 are also like terms, and we can combine them as well: subtracting 6 and 15 from both sides of the equation, we get $5x = -4 - 6 - 15$, or $5x = -25$, which simplifies further to $x = -5$.

> **Review Video: <u>Solving Equations by Combining Like Terms</u>**
> Visit mometrix.com/academy and enter code: 668506

CANCELING TERMS ON OPPOSITE SIDES OF AN EQUATION

Two terms on opposite sides of an equation can be canceled if and only if they *exactly* match each other. They must have the same variable raised to the same power and the same coefficient. For example, in the equation $3x + 2x^2 + 6 = 2x^2 - 6$, $2x^2$ appears on both sides of the equation and can be canceled, leaving $3x + 6 = -6$. The 6 on each side of the equation *cannot* be canceled, because it is added on one side of the equation and subtracted on the other. While they cannot be canceled, however, the 6 and –6 are like terms and can be combined, yielding $3x = -12$, which simplifies further to $x = -4$.

It's also important to note that the terms to be canceled must be independent terms and cannot be part of a larger term. For example, consider the equation $2(x + 6) = 3(x + 4) + 1$. We cannot cancel the x's, because even though they match each other they are part of the larger terms $2(x + 6)$ and $3(x + 4)$. We must first distribute the 2 and 3, yielding $2x + 12 = 3x + 12 + 1$. Now we see that the terms with the x's do not match, but the 12s do, and can be canceled, leaving $2x = 3x + 1$, which simplifies to $x = -1$.

PROCESS FOR MANIPULATING EQUATIONS
ISOLATING VARIABLES

To **isolate a variable** means to manipulate the equation so that the variable appears by itself on one side of the equation, and does not appear at all on the other side. Generally, an equation or inequality is considered to be solved once the variable is isolated and the other side of the equation or inequality is simplified as much as possible. In the case of a two-variable equation or inequality, only one variable needs to be isolated; it will not usually be possible to simultaneously isolate both variables.

For a linear equation—an equation in which the variable only appears raised to the first power—isolating a variable can be done by first moving all the terms with the variable to one side of the equation and all other terms to the other side. (*Moving* a term really means adding the inverse of the term to both sides; when a term is *moved* to the other side of the equation its sign is flipped.) Then combine like terms on each side. Finally, divide both sides by the coefficient of the variable, if applicable. The steps need not necessarily be done in this order, but this order will always work.

> **Review Video: <u>Solving One-Step Equations</u>**
> Visit mometrix.com/academy and enter code: 777004

EQUATIONS WITH MORE THAN ONE SOLUTION

Some types of non-linear equations, such as equations involving squares of variables, may have more than one solution. For example, the equation $x^2 = 4$ has two solutions: 2 and –2. Equations with absolute values can also have multiple solutions: $|x| = 1$ has the solutions $x = 1$ and $x = -1$.

It is also possible for a linear equation to have more than one solution, but only if the equation is true regardless of the value of the variable. In this case, the equation is considered to have infinitely many solutions, because any possible value of the variable is a solution. We know a linear equation has infinitely many solutions if when we combine like terms the variables cancel, leaving a true statement. For example, consider the equation $2(3x + 5) = x + 5(x + 2)$. Distributing, we get $6x + 10 = x + 5x + 10$; combining like terms gives $6x + 10 = 6x + 10$, and the $6x$-terms cancel to leave $10 = 10$. This is clearly true, so the original equation is true for any value of x. We could also have canceled the 10s leaving $0 = 0$, but again this is clearly true—in general if both sides of the equation match exactly, it has infinitely many solutions.

EQUATIONS WITH NO SOLUTION

Some types of non-linear equations, such as equations involving squares of variables, may have no solution. For example, the equation $x^2 = -2$ has no solutions in the real numbers, because the square of any real number must be positive. Similarly, $|x| = -1$ has no solution, because the absolute value of a number is always positive.

It is also possible for an equation to have no solution even if does not involve any powers greater than one, absolute values, or other special functions. For example, the equation $2(x + 3) + x = 3x$ has no solution. We can see that if we try to solve it: first we distribute, leaving $2x + 6 + x = 3x$. But now if we try to combine all the terms with the variable, we find that they cancel: we have $3x$ on the left and $3x$ on the right, canceling to leave us with $6 = 0$. This is clearly false. In general, whenever the variable terms in an equation cancel leaving different constants on both sides, it means that the equation has no solution. (If we are left with the *same* constant on both sides, the equation has infinitely many solutions instead.)

FEATURES OF EQUATIONS THAT REQUIRE SPECIAL TREATMENT
LINEAR EQUATIONS

A linear equation is an equation in which variables only appear by themselves: not multiplied together, not with exponents other than one, and not inside absolute value signs or any other functions. For example, the equation $x + 1 - 3x = 5 - x$ is a linear equation; while x appears multiple times, it never appears with an exponent other than one, or inside any function. The two-variable equation $2x - 3y = 5 + 2x$ is also a linear equation. In contrast, the equation $x^2 - 5 = 3x$ is *not* a linear equation, because it involves the term x^2. $\sqrt{x} = 5$ is not a linear equation, because it involves a square root. $(x - 1)^2 = 4$ is not a linear equation because even though there's no exponent on the x directly, it appears as part of an expression that is squared. The two-variable equation $x + xy - y = 5$ is not a linear equation because it includes the term xy, where two variables are multiplied together.

Linear equations can always be solved (or shown to have no solution) by combining like terms and performing simple operations on both sides of the equation. Some non-linear equations can be solved by similar methods, but others may require more advanced methods of solution, if they can be solved analytically at all.

SOLVING EQUATIONS INVOLVING ROOTS

In an equation involving roots, the first step is to isolate the term with the root, if possible, and then raise both sides of the equation to the appropriate power to eliminate it. Consider an example equation, $2\sqrt{x + 1} - 1 = 3$. In this case, begin by adding 1 to both sides, yielding $2\sqrt{x + 1} = 4$, and then dividing both sides by 2, yielding $\sqrt{x + 1} = 2$. Now square both sides, yielding $x + 1 = 4$. Finally, subtracting 1 from both sides yields $x = 3$.

Squaring both sides of an equation may, however, yield a spurious solution—a solution to the squared equation that is *not* a solution of the original equation. It's therefore necessary to plug the solution back into the original equation to make sure it works. In this case, it does: $2\sqrt{3 + 1} - 1 = 2\sqrt{4} - 1 = 2(2) - 1 = 4 - 1 = 3$.

The same procedure applies for other roots as well. For example, given the equation $3 + \sqrt[3]{2x} = 5$, we can first subtract 3 from both sides, yielding $\sqrt[3]{2x} = 2$ and isolating the root. Raising both sides to the third power yields $2x = 2^3$; i.e., $2x = 8$. We can now divide both sides by 2 to get $x = 4$.

Review Video: Solving Equations Involving Roots
Visit mometrix.com/academy and enter code: 297670

SOLVING EQUATIONS WITH EXPONENTS

To solve an equation involving an exponent, the first step is to isolate the variable with the exponent. We can then take the appropriate root of both sides to eliminate the exponent. For instance, for the equation $2x^3 + 17 = 5x^3 - 7$, we can subtract $5x^3$ from both sides to get $-3x^3 + 17 = -7$, and then subtract 17 from both sides to get $-3x^3 = -24$. Finally, we can divide both sides by –3 to get $x^3 = 8$. Finally, we can take the cube root of both sides to get $x = \sqrt[3]{8} = 2$.

One important but often overlooked point is that equations with an exponent greater than 1 may have more than one answer. The solution to $x^2 = 9$ isn't simply $x = 3$; it's $x = \pm 3$ (that is, $x = 3$ or $x = -3$). For a slightly more complicated example, consider the equation $(x - 1)^2 - 1 = 3$. Adding 1 to both sides yields $(x - 1)^2 = 4$; taking the square root of both sides yields $x - 1 = 2$. We can then add 1 to both sides to get $x = 3$. However, there's a second solution. We also have the possibility that $x - 1 = -2$, in which case $x = -1$. Both $x = 3$ and $x = -1$ are valid solutions, as can be verified by substituting them both into the original equation.

> **Review Video: Solving Equations with Exponents**
> Visit mometrix.com/academy and enter code: 514557

SOLVING EQUATIONS WITH ABSOLUTE VALUES

When solving an equation with an absolute value, the first step is to isolate the absolute value term. We then consider two possibilities: when the expression inside the absolute value is positive or when it is negative. In the former case, the expression in the absolute value equals the expression on the other side of the equation; in the latter, it equals the additive inverse of that expression—the expression times negative one. We consider each case separately and finally check for spurious solutions.

For instance, consider solving $|2x - 1| + x = 5$ for x. We can first isolate the absolute value by moving the x to the other side: $|2x - 1| = -x + 5$. Now, we have two possibilities. First, that $2x - 1$ is positive, and hence $2x - 1 = -x + 5$. Rearranging and combining like terms yields $3x = 6$, and hence $x = 2$. The other possibility is that $2x - 1$ is negative, and hence $2x - 1 = -(-x + 5) = x - 5$. In this case, rearranging and combining like terms yields $x = -4$. Substituting $x = 2$ and $x = -4$ back into the original equation, we see that they are both valid solutions.

Note that the absolute value of a sum or difference applies to the sum or difference as a whole, not to the individual terms; in general, $|2x - 1|$ is not equal to $|2x + 1|$ or to $|2x| - 1$.

SPURIOUS SOLUTIONS

A **spurious solution** may arise when we square both sides of an equation as a step in solving it or under certain other operations on the equation. It is a solution to the squared or otherwise modified equation that is *not* a solution of the original equation. To identify a spurious solution, it's useful when you solve an equation involving roots or absolute values to plug the solution back into the original equation to make sure it's valid.

CHOOSING WHICH VARIABLE TO ISOLATE IN TWO-VARIABLE EQUATIONS

Similar to methods for a one-variable equation, solving a two-variable equation involves isolating a variable: manipulating the equation so that a variable appears by itself on one side of the equation, and not at all on the other side. However, in a two-variable equation, you will usually only be able to isolate one of the variables; the other variable may appear on the other side along with constant terms, or with exponents or other functions.

Often one variable will be much more easily isolated than the other, and therefore that's the variable you should choose. If one variable appears with various exponents, and the other is only raised to the first power, the latter variable is the one to isolate: given the equation $a^2 + 2b = a^3 + b + 3$, the b only appears to the first power, whereas a appears squared and cubed, so b is the variable that can be solved for: combining like terms and isolating the b on the left side of the equation, we get $b = a^3 - a^2 + 3$. If both variables are equally easy to isolate, then it's best to isolate the dependent variable, if one is defined; if the two variables are x and y, the convention is that y is the dependent variable.

> **Review Video: Solving Equations with Variables on Both Sides**
> Visit mometrix.com/academy and enter code: 402497

Graphing Equations

GRAPHICAL SOLUTIONS TO EQUATIONS

When equations are shown graphically, they are usually shown on a **Cartesian coordinate plane**. The Cartesian coordinate plane consists of two number lines placed perpendicular to each other and intersecting at the zero point, also known as the origin. The horizontal number line is known as the x-axis, with positive values to the right of the origin, and negative values to the left of the origin. The vertical number line is known as the y-axis, with positive values above the origin, and negative values below the origin. Any point on the plane can be identified by an ordered pair in the form (x, y), called coordinates. The x-value of the coordinate is called the abscissa, and the y-value of the coordinate is called the ordinate. The two number lines divide the plane into **four quadrants**: I, II, III, and IV.

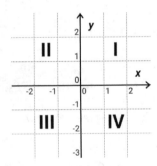

Note that in quadrant I $x > 0$ and $y > 0$, in quadrant II $x < 0$ and $y > 0$, in quadrant III $x < 0$ and $y < 0$, and in quadrant IV $x > 0$ and $y < 0$.

Recall that if the value of the slope of a line is positive, the line slopes upward from left to right. If the value of the slope is negative, the line slopes downward from left to right. If the y-coordinates are the same for two points on a line, the slope is 0 and the line is a **horizontal line**. If the x-coordinates are the same for two points on a line, there is no slope and the line is a **vertical line**. Two or more lines that have equivalent slopes are **parallel lines**. **Perpendicular lines** have slopes that are negative reciprocals of each other, such as $\frac{a}{b}$ and $\frac{-b}{a}$.

> **Review Video: Cartesian Coordinate Plane and Graphing**
> Visit mometrix.com/academy and enter code: 115173

GRAPHING EQUATIONS IN TWO VARIABLES

One way of graphing an equation in two variables is to plot enough points to get an idea for its shape and then draw the appropriate curve through those points. A point can be plotted by substituting in a value for one variable and solving for the other. If the equation is linear, we only need two points and can then draw a straight line between them.

For example, consider the equation $y = 2x - 1$. This is a linear equation—both variables only appear raised to the first power—so we only need two points. When $x = 0$, $y = 2(0) - 1 = -1$. When $x = 2$, $y = 2(2) - 1 = 3$. We can therefore choose the points $(0, -1)$ and $(2, 3)$, and draw a line between them:

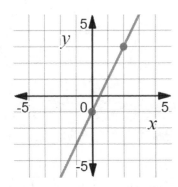

Inequalities

WORKING WITH INEQUALITIES

Commonly in algebra and other upper-level fields of math you find yourself working with mathematical expressions that do not equal each other. The statement comparing such expressions with symbols such as $<$ (less than) or $>$ (greater than) is called an *inequality*. An example of an inequality is $7x > 5$. To solve for x, simply divide both sides by 7 and the solution is shown to be $x > \frac{5}{7}$. Graphs of the solution set of inequalities are represented on a number line. Open circles are used to show that an expression approaches a number but is never quite equal to that number.

> **Review Video: <u>Solving Multi-Step Inequalities</u>**
> Visit mometrix.com/academy and enter code: 347842
>
> **Review Video: <u>Solving Inequalities Using All 4 Basic Operations</u>**
> Visit mometrix.com/academy and enter code: 401111

Conditional inequalities are those with certain values for the variable that will make the condition true and other values for the variable where the condition will be false. **Absolute inequalities** can have any real number as the value for the variable to make the condition true, while there is no real number value for the variable that will make the condition false. Solving inequalities is done by following the same rules for solving equations with the exception that when multiplying or dividing by a negative number the direction of the inequality sign must be flipped or reversed. **Double**

inequalities are situations where two inequality statements apply to the same variable expression. Example: $-c < ax + b < c$.

Review Video: Conditional and Absolute Inequalities
Visit mometrix.com/academy and enter code: 980164

DETERMINING SOLUTIONS TO INEQUALITIES

To determine whether a coordinate is a solution of an inequality, you can substitute the values of the coordinate into the inequality, simplify, and check whether the resulting statement holds true. For instance, to determine whether $(-2,4)$ is a solution of the inequality $y \geq -2x + 3$, substitute the values into the inequality, $4 \geq -2(-2) + 3$. Simplify the right side of the inequality and the result is $4 \geq 7$, which is a false statement. Therefore, the coordinate is not a solution of the inequality. You can also use this method to determine which part of the graph of an inequality is shaded. The graph of $y \geq -2x + 3$ includes the solid line $y = -2x + 3$ and, since it excludes the point $(-2,4)$ to the left of the line, it is shaded to the right of the line.

Review Video: Graphing Linear Inequalities
Visit mometrix.com/academy and enter code: 439421

FLIPPING INEQUALITY SIGNS

When given an inequality, we can always turn the entire inequality around, swapping the two sides of the inequality and changing the inequality sign. For instance, $x + 2 > 2x - 3$ is equivalent to $2x - 3 < x + 2$. Aside from that, normally the inequality does not change if we carry out the same operation on both sides of the inequality. There is, however, one principal exception: if we *multiply* or *divide* both sides of the inequality by a *negative number*, the inequality is flipped. For example, if we take the inequality $-2x < 6$ and divide both sides by -2, the inequality flips and we are left with $x > -3$. This *only* applies to multiplication and division, and only with negative numbers. Multiplying or dividing both sides by a positive number, or adding or subtracting any number regardless of sign, does not flip the inequality. Another special case that flips the inequality sign is when reciprocals are used. For instance, $3 > 2$ but the relation of the reciprocals is $\frac{1}{2} < \frac{1}{3}$.

COMPOUND INEQUALITIES

A **compound inequality** is an equality that consists of two inequalities combined with *and* or *or*. The two components of a proper compound inequality must be of opposite type: that is, one must be greater than (or greater than or equal to), the other less than (or less than or equal to). For instance, "$x + 1 < 2$ or $x + 1 > 3$" is a compound inequality, as is "$2x \geq 4$ and $2x \leq 6$." An *and* inequality can be written more compactly by having one inequality on each side of the common part: "$2x \geq 1$ and $2x \leq 6$," can also be written as $1 \leq 2x \leq 6$.

In order for the compound inequality to be meaningful, the two parts of an *and* inequality must overlap; otherwise, no numbers satisfy the inequality. On the other hand, if the two parts of an *or* inequality overlap, then *all* numbers satisfy the inequality and as such the inequality is usually not meaningful.

Solving a compound inequality requires solving each part separately. For example, given the compound inequality "$x + 1 < 2$ or $x + 1 > 3$," the first inequality, $x + 1 < 2$, reduces to $x < 1$, and the second part, $x + 1 > 3$, reduces to $x > 2$, so the whole compound inequality can be written as "$x < 1$ or $x > 2$." Similarly, $1 \leq 2x \leq 6$ can be solved by dividing each term by 2, yielding $\frac{1}{2} \leq x \leq 3$.

> **Review Video: Compound Inequalities**
> Visit mometrix.com/academy and enter code: 786318

SOLVING INEQUALITIES INVOLVING ABSOLUTE VALUES

To solve an inequality involving an absolute value, first isolate the term with the absolute value. Then proceed to treat the two cases separately as with an absolute value equation, but flipping the inequality in the case where the expression in the absolute value is negative (since that essentially involves multiplying both sides by –1.) The two cases are then combined into a compound inequality; if the absolute value is on the greater side of the inequality, then it is an *or* compound inequality, if on the lesser side, then it's an *and*.

Consider the inequality $2 + |x - 1| \geq 3$. We can isolate the absolute value term by subtracting 2 from both sides: $|x - 1| \geq 1$. Now, we're left with the two cases $x - 1 \geq 1$ or $x - 1 \leq -1$: note that in the latter, negative case, the inequality is flipped. $x - 1 \geq 1$ reduces to $x \geq 2$, and $x - 1 \leq -1$ reduces to $x \leq 0$. Since in the inequality $|x - 1| \geq 1$ the absolute value is on the greater side, the two cases combine into an *or* compound inequality, so the final, solved inequality is "$x \leq 0$ or $x \geq 2$."

> **Review Video: Solving Absolute Value Inequalities**
> Visit mometrix.com/academy and enter code: 997008

SOLVING INEQUALITIES INVOLVING SQUARE ROOTS

Solving an inequality with a square root involves two parts. First, we solve the inequality as if it were an equation, isolating the square root and then squaring both sides of the equation. Second, we restrict the solution to the set of values of x for which the value inside the square root sign is non-negative.

For example, in the inequality, $\sqrt{x - 2} + 1 < 5$, we can isolate the square root by subtracting 1 from both sides, yielding $\sqrt{x - 2} < 4$. Squaring both sides of the inequality yields $x - 2 < 16$, so $x < 18$. Since we can't take the square root of a negative number, we also require the part inside the square root to be non-negative. In this case, that means $x - 2 \geq 0$. Adding 2 to both sides of the inequality yields $x \geq 2$. Our final answer is a compound inequality combining the two simple inequalities: $x \geq 2$ and $x < 18$, or $2 \leq x < 18$.

Note that we only get a compound inequality if the two simple inequalities are in opposite directions; otherwise, we take the one that is more restrictive.

The same technique can be used for other even roots, such as fourth roots. It is *not*, however, used for cube roots or other odd roots—negative numbers *do* have cube roots, so the condition that the quantity inside the root sign cannot be negative does not apply.

> **Review Video: Solving Inequalities Involving Square Roots**
> Visit mometrix.com/academy and enter code: 800288

SPECIAL CIRCUMSTANCES

Sometimes an inequality involving an absolute value or an even exponent is true for all values of x, and we don't need to do any further work to solve it. This is true if the inequality, once the absolute value or exponent term is isolated, says that term is greater than a negative number (or greater than or equal to zero). Since an absolute value or a number raised to an even exponent is *always* non-negative, this inequality is always true.

GRAPHICAL SOLUTIONS TO INEQUALITIES
GRAPHING SIMPLE INEQUALITIES

To graph a simple inequality, we first mark on the number line the value that signifies the end point of the inequality. If the inequality is strict (involves a less than or greater than), we use a hollow circle; if it is not strict (less than or equal to or greater than or equal to), we use a solid circle. We then fill in the part of the number line that satisfies the inequality: to the left of the marked point for less than (or less than or equal to), to the right for greater than (or greater than or equal to).

For example, we would graph the inequality $x < 5$ by putting a hollow circle at 5 and filling in the part of the line to the left:

GRAPHING COMPOUND INEQUALITIES

To graph a compound inequality, we fill in both parts of the inequality for an *or* inequality, or the overlap between them for an *and* inequality. More specifically, we start by plotting the endpoints of each inequality on the number line. For an *or* inequality, we then fill in the appropriate side of the line for each inequality. Typically, the two component inequalities do not overlap, which means the shaded part is *outside* the two points. For an *and* inequality, we instead fill in the part of the line that meets both inequalities.

For the inequality "$x \le -3$ or $x > 4$," we first put a solid circle at –3 and a hollow circle at 4. We then fill the parts of the line *outside* these circles:

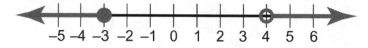

GRAPHING INEQUALITIES INCLUDING ABSOLUTE VALUES

An inequality with an absolute value can be converted to a compound inequality. To graph the inequality, first convert it to a compound inequality, and then graph that normally. If the absolute value is on the greater side of the inequality, we end up with an *or* inequality; we plot the endpoints of the inequality on the number line and fill in the part of the line *outside* those points. If the absolute value is on the smaller side of the inequality, we end up with an *and* inequality; we plot the endpoints of the inequality on the number line and fill in the part of the line *between* those points.

For example, the inequality $|x + 1| \ge 4$ can be rewritten as $x \ge 3$ or $x \le -5$. We place solid circles at the points 3 and –5 and fill in the part of the line *outside* them:

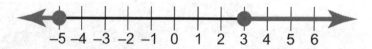

GRAPHING INEQUALITIES IN TWO VARIABLES

To graph an inequality in two variables, we first graph the border of the inequality. This means graphing the equation that we get if we replace the inequality sign with an equals sign. If the

38

inequality is strict (> or <), we graph the border with a dashed or dotted line; if it is not strict (≥ or ≤), we use a solid line. We can then test any point not on the border to see if it satisfies the inequality. If it does, we shade in that side of the border; if not, we shade in the other side. As an example, consider $y > 2x + 2$. To graph this inequality, we first graph the border, $y = 2x + 2$. Since it is a strict inequality, we use a dashed line. Then, we choose a test point. This can be any point not on the border; in this case, we will choose the origin, $(0,0)$. (This makes the calculation easy and is generally a good choice unless the border passes through the origin.) Putting this into the original inequality, we get $0 > 2(0) + 2$, i.e., $0 > 2$. This is *not* true, so we shade in the side of the border that does *not* include the point $(0,0)$:

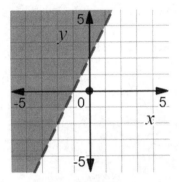

GRAPHING COMPOUND INEQUALITIES IN TWO VARIABLES

One way to graph a compound inequality in two variables is to first graph each of the component inequalities. For an *and* inequality, we then shade in only the parts where the two graphs overlap; for an *or* inequality, we shade in any region that pertains to either of the individual inequalities.

Consider the graph of "$y \geq x - 1$ and $y \leq -x$":

We first shade in the individual inequalities:

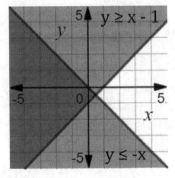

Now, since the compound inequality has an *and*, we only leave shaded the overlap—the part that pertains to *both* inequalities:

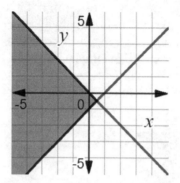

If instead the inequality had been "$y \geq x - 1$ or $y \leq -x$," our final graph would involve the *total* shaded area:

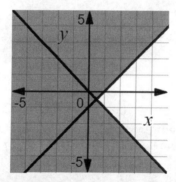

Review Video: <u>Graphing Solutions to Inequalities</u>
Visit mometrix.com/academy and enter code: 391281

Systems of Equations

SOLVING SYSTEMS OF EQUATIONS

A **system of equations** is a set of simultaneous equations that all use the same variables. A solution to a system of equations must be true for each equation in the system. **Consistent systems** are those with at least one solution. **Inconsistent systems** are systems of equations that have no solution.

Review Video: <u>Solving Systems of Linear Equations</u>
Visit mometrix.com/academy and enter code: 746745

SUBSTITUTION

To solve a system of linear equations by **substitution**, start with the easier equation and solve for one of the variables. Express this variable in terms of the other variable. Substitute this expression in the other equation and solve for the other variable. The solution should be expressed in the form (x, y). Substitute the values into both of the original equations to check your answer. Consider the following system of equations:

$$x + 6y = 15$$
$$3x - 12y = 18$$

40

Solving the first equation for x: $x = 15 - 6y$

Substitute this value in place of x in the second equation, and solve for y:

$$3(15 - 6y) - 12y = 18$$
$$45 - 18y - 12y = 18$$
$$30y = 27$$
$$y = \frac{27}{30} = \frac{9}{10} = 0.9$$

Plug this value for y back into the first equation to solve for x:

$$x = 15 - 6(0.9) = 15 - 5.4 = 9.6$$

Check both equations if you have time:

$$9.6 + 6(0.9) = 15 \qquad 3(9.6) - 12(0.9) = 18$$
$$9.6 + 5.4 = 15 \qquad 28.8 - 10.8 = 18$$
$$15 = 15 \qquad 18 = 18$$

Therefore, the solution is (9.6,0.9).

> **Review Video: The Substitution Method**
> Visit mometrix.com/academy and enter code: 565151
>
> **Review Video: Substitution and Elimination**
> Visit mometrix.com/academy and enter code: 958611

ELIMINATION

To solve a system of equations using **elimination**, begin by rewriting both equations in standard form $Ax + By = C$. Check to see if the coefficients of one pair of like variables add to zero. If not, multiply one or both of the equations by a non-zero number to make one set of like variables add to zero. Add the two equations to solve for one of the variables. Substitute this value into one of the original equations to solve for the other variable. Check your work by substituting into the other equation. Now, let's look at solving the following system using the elimination method:

$$5x + 6y = 4$$
$$x + 2y = 4$$

If we multiply the second equation by -3, we can eliminate the y-terms:

$$5x + 6y = 4$$
$$-3x - 6y = -12$$

Add the equations together and solve for x:

$$2x = -8$$
$$x = \frac{-8}{2} = -4$$

Plug the value for x back in to either of the original equations and solve for y:

$$-4 + 2y = 4$$
$$y = \frac{4+4}{2} = 4$$

Check both equations if you have time:

$$5(-4) + 6(4) = 4 \qquad\qquad -4 + 2(4) = 4$$
$$-20 + 24 = 4 \qquad\qquad -4 + 8 = 4$$
$$4 = 4 \qquad\qquad 4 = 4$$

Therefore, the solution is $(-4,4)$.

> **Review Video: The Elimination Method**
> Visit mometrix.com/academy and enter code: 449121

GRAPHICALLY

To solve a system of linear equations **graphically**, plot both equations on the same graph. The solution of the equations is the point where both lines cross. If the lines do not cross (are parallel), then there is **no solution**.

For example, consider the following system of equations:

$$y = 2x + 7$$
$$y = -x + 1$$

Since these equations are given in slope-intercept form, they are easy to graph; the y-intercepts of the lines are $(0,7)$ and $(0,1)$. The respective slopes are 2 and –1, thus the graphs look like this:

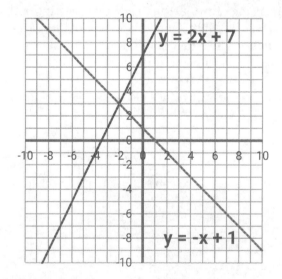

The two lines intersect at the point $(-2,3)$, thus this is the solution to the system of equations.

Solving a system graphically is generally only practical if both coordinates of the solution are integers; otherwise the intersection will lie between gridlines on the graph and the coordinates will be difficult or impossible to determine exactly. It also helps if, as in this example, the equations are in slope-intercept form or some other form that makes them easy to graph. Otherwise, another method of solution (by substitution or elimination) is likely to be more useful.

Review Video: Solving Systems by Graphing
Visit mometrix.com/academy and enter code: 634812

SOLVING SYSTEMS OF EQUATIONS USING THE TRACE FEATURE

Using the trace feature on a calculator requires that you rewrite each equation, isolating the y-variable on one side of the equal sign. Enter both equations in the graphing calculator and plot the graphs simultaneously. Use the trace cursor to find where the two lines cross. Use the zoom feature if necessary to obtain more accurate results. Always check your answer by substituting into the original equations. The trace method is likely to be less accurate than other methods due to the resolution of graphing calculators but is a useful tool to provide an approximate answer.

Advanced Systems of Equations

SOLVING A SYSTEM OF EQUATIONS CONSISTING OF A LINEAR EQUATION AND A QUADRATIC EQUATION

ALGEBRAICALLY

Generally, the simplest way to solve a system of equations consisting of a linear equation and a quadratic equation algebraically is through the method of substitution. One possible strategy is to solve the linear equation for y and then substitute that expression into the quadratic equation. After expansion and combining like terms, this will result in a new quadratic equation for x, which, like all quadratic equations, may have zero, one, or two solutions. Plugging each solution for x back into one of the original equations will then produce the corresponding value of y.

For example, consider the following system of equations:

$$x + y = 1$$
$$y = (x + 3)^2 - 2$$

We can solve the linear equation for y to yield $y = -x + 1$. Substituting this expression into the quadratic equation produces $-x + 1 = (x + 3)^2 - 2$. We can simplify this equation:

$$-x + 1 = (x + 3)^2 - 2$$
$$-x + 1 = x^2 + 6x + 9 - 2$$
$$-x + 1 = x^2 + 6x + 7$$
$$0 = x^2 + 7x + 6$$

This quadratic equation can be factored as $(x + 1)(x + 6) = 0$. It therefore has two solutions: $x_1 = -1$ and $x_2 = -6$. Plugging each of these back into the original linear equation yields $y_1 = -x_1 + 1 = -(-1) + 1 = 2$ and $y_2 = -x_2 + 1 = -(-6) + 1 = 7$. Thus, this system of equations has two solutions, $(-1,2)$ and $(-6,7)$.

It may help to check your work by putting each x- and y-value back into the original equations and verifying that they do provide a solution.

GRAPHICALLY

To solve a system of equations consisting of a linear equation and a quadratic equation graphically, plot both equations on the same graph. The linear equation will, of course, produce a straight line, while the quadratic equation will produce a parabola. These two graphs will intersect at zero, one, or two points; each point of intersection is a solution of the system.

For example, consider the following system of equations:

$$y = -2x + 2$$
$$y = -2x^2 + 4x + 2$$

The linear equation describes a line with a y-intercept of $(0,2)$ and a slope of -2.

To graph the quadratic equation, we can first find the vertex of the parabola: the x-coordinate of the vertex is $h = -\frac{b}{2a} = -\frac{4}{2(-2)} = 1$, and the y-coordinate is $k = -2(1)^2 + 4(1) + 2 = 4$. Thus, the vertex lies at $(1,4)$. To get a feel for the rest of the parabola, we can plug in a few more values of x to find more points; by putting in $x = 2$ and $x = 3$ in the quadratic equation, we find that the points $(2,2)$ and $(3,-4)$ lie on the parabola; by symmetry, so must $(0,2)$ and $(-1,-4)$. We can now plot both equations:

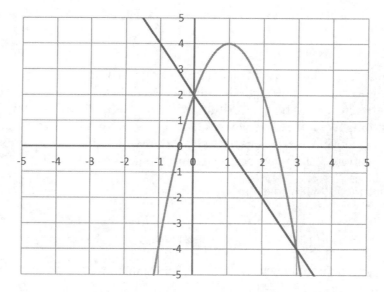

These two curves intersect at the points $(0,2)$ and $(3,-4)$, thus these are the solutions of the equation.

> **Review Video: <u>Solving a System of Equations Consisting of a Linear Equation and Quadratic Equations</u>**
> Visit mometrix.com/academy and enter code: 194870

Calculations Using Points

Sometimes you need to perform calculations using only points on a graph as input data. Using points, you can determine what the **midpoint** and **distance** are. If you know the equation for a line, you can calculate the distance between the line and the point.

To find the **midpoint** of two points (x_1, y_1) and (x_2, y_2), average the x-coordinates to get the x-coordinate of the midpoint, and average the y-coordinates to get the y-coordinate of the midpoint. The formula is: $\left(\frac{x_1+x_2}{2}, \frac{y_1+y_2}{2}\right)$.

The **distance** between two points is the same as the length of the hypotenuse of a right triangle with the two given points as endpoints, and the two sides of the right triangle parallel to the x-axis and y-axis, respectively. The length of the segment parallel to the x-axis is the difference between the x-coordinates of the two points. The length of the segment parallel to the y-axis is the difference between the y-coordinates of the two points. Use the Pythagorean theorem $a^2 + b^2 = c^2$ or $c = \sqrt{a^2 + b^2}$ to find the distance. The formula is $d = \sqrt{(x_2 - x_1)^2 + (y_2 - y_1)^2}$.

When a line is in the format $Ax + By + C = 0$, where A, B, and C are coefficients, you can use a point (x_1, y_1) not on the line and apply the formula $d = \frac{|Ax_1 + By_1 + C|}{\sqrt{A^2 + B^2}}$ to find the distance between the line and the point (x_1, y_1).

> **Review Video: Calculations Using Points on a Graph**
> Visit mometrix.com/academy and enter code: 883228

Polynomials

MONOMIALS AND POLYNOMIALS

A **monomial** is a single constant, variable, or product of constants and variables, such as 7, x, $2x$, or $x^3 y$. There will never be addition or subtraction symbols in a monomial. Like monomials have like variables, but they may have different coefficients. **Polynomials** are algebraic expressions that use addition and subtraction to combine two or more monomials. Two terms make a **binomial**, three terms make a **trinomial**, etc. The **degree of a monomial** is the sum of the exponents of the variables. The **degree of a polynomial** is the highest degree of any individual term.

> **Review Video: Polynomials**
> Visit mometrix.com/academy and enter code: 305005

SIMPLIFYING POLYNOMIALS

Simplifying polynomials requires combining like terms. The like terms in a polynomial expression are those that have the same variable raised to the same power. It is often helpful to connect the like terms with arrows or lines in order to separate them from the other monomials. Once you have determined the like terms, you can rearrange the polynomial by placing them together. Remember to include the sign that is in front of each term. Once the like terms are placed together, you can apply each operation and simplify. When adding and subtracting polynomials, only add and subtract the **coefficient**, or the number part; the variable and exponent stay the same.

ADD POLYNOMIALS

To add polynomials, you need to add like terms. These terms have the same variable part. An example is $4x^2$ and $3x^2$ have x^2 terms. To find the sum of like terms, find the sum of the coefficients. Then, keep the same variable part. You can use the distributive property to distribute the plus sign to each term of the polynomial. For example:

$(4x^2 - 5x + 7) + (3x^2 + 2x + 1) =$
$(4x^2 - 5x + 7) + 3x^2 + 2x + 1 =$
$(4x^2 + 3x^2) + (-5x + 2x) + (7 + 1) =$
$7x^2 - 3x + 8$

Subtract Polynomials

To subtract polynomials, you need to subtract like terms. To find the difference of like terms, find the difference of the coefficients. Then, keep the same variable part. You can use the distributive property to distribute the minus sign to each term of the polynomial. For example:

$(-2x^2 - x + 5) - (3x^2 - 4x + 1) =$
$(-2x^2 - x + 5) - 3x^2 + 4x - 1 =$
$(-2x^2 - 3x^2) + (-x + 4x) + (5 - 1) =$
$-5x^2 + 3x + 4$

Review Video: Adding and Subtracting Polynomials
Visit mometrix.com/academy and enter code: 124088

Multiplying Polynomials

In general, multiplying polynomials is done by multiplying each term in one polynomial by each term in the other and adding the results. In the specific case for multiplying binomials, there is a useful acronym, FOIL, that can help you make sure to cover each combination of terms. The **FOIL method** for $(Ax + By)(Cx + Dy)$ would be:

F	Multiply the *first* terms of each binomial	$(\overset{first}{Ax} + By)(\overset{first}{Cx} + Dy)$	ACx^2
O	Multiply the *outer* terms	$(\overset{outer}{Ax} + By)(Cx + \overset{outer}{Dy})$	$ADxy$
I	Multiply the *inner* terms	$(Ax + \overset{inner}{By})(\overset{inner}{Cx} + Dy)$	$BCxy$
L	Multiply the *last* terms of each binomial	$(Ax + \overset{last}{By})(Cx + \overset{last}{Dy})$	BDy^2

Then, add up the result of each and combine like terms: $ACx^2 + (AD + BC)xy + BDy^2$.

For example, using the FOIL method on binomials $(x + 2)$ and $(x - 3)$:

First: $(\boxed{x} + 2)(\boxed{x} + (-3)) \rightarrow (x)(x) = x^2$
Outer: $(\boxed{x} + 2)(x + \boxed{(-3)}) \rightarrow (x)(-3) = -3x$
Inner: $(x + \boxed{2})(\boxed{x} + (-3)) \rightarrow (2)(x) = 2x$
Last: $(x + \boxed{2})(x + \boxed{(-3)}) \rightarrow (2)(-3) = -6$

This results in: $(x^2) + (-3x) + (2x) + (-6)$

Combine like terms: $x^2 + (-3 + 2)x + (-6) = x^2 - x - 6$

Review Video: Multiplying Terms Using the FOIL Method
Visit mometrix.com/academy and enter code: 854792

Dividing Polynomials

Use long division to divide a polynomial by either a monomial or another polynomial of equal or lesser degree.

When **dividing by a monomial**, divide each term of the polynomial by the monomial.

When **dividing by a polynomial**, begin by arranging the terms of each polynomial in order of one variable. You may arrange in ascending or descending order, but be consistent with both polynomials. To get the first term of the quotient, divide the first term of the dividend by the first term of the divisor. Multiply the first term of the quotient by the entire divisor and subtract that product from the dividend. Repeat for the second and successive terms until you either get a remainder of zero or a remainder whose degree is less than the degree of the divisor. If the quotient has a remainder, write the answer as a mixed expression in the form:

$$\text{quotient} + \frac{\text{remainder}}{\text{divisor}}$$

For example, we can evaluate the following expression in the same way as long division:

$$\frac{x^3 - 3x^2 - 2x + 5}{x - 5}$$

$$
\begin{array}{r}
x^2 + 2x + 8 \\
x - 5 \overline{)\, x^3 - 3x^2 - 2x + 5} \\
-(x^3 - 5x^2) \\
\hline
2x^2 - 2x \\
-(2x^2 - 10x) \\
\hline
8x + 5 \\
-(8x - 40) \\
\hline
45
\end{array}
$$

$$\frac{x^3 - 3x^2 - 2x + 5}{x - 5} = x^2 + 2x + 8 + \frac{45}{x - 5}$$

When **factoring** a polynomial, first check for a common monomial factor, that is, look to see if each coefficient has a common factor or if each term has an x in it. If the factor is a trinomial but not a perfect trinomial square, look for a factorable form, such as one of these:

$$x^2 + (a + b)x + ab = (x + a)(x + b)$$
$$(ac)x^2 + (ad + bc)x + bd = (ax + b)(cx + d)$$

For factors with four terms, look for groups to factor. Once you have found the factors, write the original polynomial as the product of all the factors. Make sure all of the polynomial factors are prime. Monomial factors may be *prime* or *composite*. Check your work by multiplying the factors to make sure you get the original polynomial.

Below are patterns of some special products to remember to help make factoring easier:

- Perfect trinomial squares: $x^2 + 2xy + y^2 = (x + y)^2$ or $x^2 - 2xy + y^2 = (x - y)^2$
- Difference between two squares: $x^2 - y^2 = (x + y)(x - y)$
- Sum of two cubes: $x^3 + y^3 = (x + y)(x^2 - xy + y^2)$
    - Note: the second factor is *not* the same as a perfect trinomial square, so do not try to factor it further.
- Difference between two cubes: $x^3 - y^3 = (x - y)(x^2 + xy + y^2)$

o Again, the second factor is *not* the same as a perfect trinomial square.

- Perfect cubes: $x^3 + 3x^2y + 3xy^2 + y^3 = (x + y)^3$ and $x^3 - 3x^2y + 3xy^2 - y^3 = (x - y)^3$

Rational Expressions

Rational expressions are fractions with polynomials in both the numerator and the denominator; the value of the polynomial in the denominator cannot be equal to zero. Be sure to keep track of values that make the denominator of the original expression zero as the final result inherits the same restrictions. For example, a denominator of $x - 3$ indicates that the expression is not defined when $x = 3$ and, as such, regardless of any operations done to the expression, it remains undefined there.

To **add or subtract** rational expressions, first find the common denominator, then rewrite each fraction as an equivalent fraction with the common denominator. Finally, add or subtract the numerators to get the numerator of the answer, and keep the common denominator as the denominator of the answer.

When **multiplying** rational expressions, factor each polynomial and cancel like factors (a factor which appears in both the numerator and the denominator). Then, multiply all remaining factors in the numerator to get the numerator of the product, and multiply the remaining factors in the denominator to get the denominator of the product. Remember: cancel entire factors, not individual terms.

To **divide** rational expressions, take the reciprocal of the divisor (the rational expression you are dividing by) and multiply by the dividend.

> **Review Video: Rational Expressions**
> Visit mometrix.com/academy and enter code: 415183

SIMPLIFYING RATIONAL EXPRESSIONS

To simplify a rational expression, factor the numerator and denominator completely. Factors that are the same and appear in the numerator and denominator have a ratio of 1. For example, look at the following expression:

$$\frac{x - 1}{1 - x^2}$$

The denominator, $(1 - x^2)$, is a difference of squares. It can be factored as $(1 - x)(1 + x)$. The factor $1 - x$ and the numerator $x - 1$ are opposites and have a ratio of –1. Rewrite the numerator as $-1(1 - x)$. So, the rational expression can be simplified as follows:

$$\frac{x - 1}{1 - x^2} = \frac{-1(1 - x)}{(1 - x)(1 + x)} = \frac{-1}{1 + x}$$

Note that since the original expression is only defined for $x \neq \{-1, 1\}$, the simplified expression has the same restrictions.

> **Review Video: Reducing Rational Expressions**
> Visit mometrix.com/academy and enter code: 788868

Quadratics

SOLVING QUADRATIC EQUATIONS

Quadratic equations are a special set of trinomials of the form $y = ax^2 + bx + c$ that occur commonly in math and real-world applications. The **roots** of a quadratic equation are the solutions that satisfy the equation when $y = 0$; in other words, where the graph touches the x-axis. There are several ways to determine these solutions including using the quadratic formula, factoring, completing the square, and graphing the function.

> **Review Video: Quadratic Equations Overview**
> Visit mometrix.com/academy and enter code: 476276
>
> **Review Video: Solutions of a Quadratic Equation on a Graph**
> Visit mometrix.com/academy and enter code: 328231

QUADRATIC FORMULA

The **quadratic formula** is used to solve quadratic equations when other methods are more difficult. To use the quadratic formula to solve a quadratic equation, begin by rewriting the equation in standard form $ax^2 + bx + c = 0$, where a, b, and c are coefficients. Once you have identified the values of the coefficients, substitute those values into the quadratic formula

$$x = \frac{-b \pm \sqrt{b^2 - 4ac}}{2a}$$

Evaluate the equation and simplify the expression. Again, check each root by substituting into the original equation. In the quadratic formula, the portion of the formula under the radical ($b^2 - 4ac$) is called the **discriminant**. If the discriminant is zero, there is only one root: $-\frac{b}{2a}$. If the discriminant is positive, there are two different real roots. If the discriminant is negative, there are no real roots; you will instead find complex roots. Often these solutions don't make sense in context and are ignored.

> **Review Video: Using the Quadratic Formula**
> Visit mometrix.com/academy and enter code: 163102

FACTORING

To solve a quadratic equation by factoring, begin by rewriting the equation in standard form, $x^2 + bx + c = 0$. Remember that the goal of factoring is to find numbers f and g such that $(x + f)(x + g) = x^2 + (f + g)x + fg$, in other words $(f + g) = b$ and $fg = c$. This can be a really useful method when b and c are integers. Determine the factors of c and look for pairs that could sum to b.

For example, consider finding the roots of $x^2 + 6x - 16 = 0$. The factors of -16 include, -4 and 4, -8 and 2, -2 and 8, -1 and 16, and 1 and -16. The factors that sum to 6 are -2 and 8. Write these factors as the product of two binomials, $0 = (x - 2)(x + 8)$. Finally, since these binomials multiply together to equal zero, set them each equal to zero and solve each for x. This results in $x - 2 = 0$, which simplifies to $x = 2$ and $x + 8 = 0$, which simplifies to $x = -8$. Therefore, the roots of the equation are 2 and -8.

> **Review Video: Factoring Quadratic Equations**
> Visit mometrix.com/academy and enter code: 336566

COMPLETING THE SQUARE

One way to find the roots of a quadratic equation is to find a way to manipulate it such that it follows the form of a perfect square ($x^2 + 2px + p^2$) by adding and subtracting a constant. This process is called **completing the square**. In other words, if you are given a quadratic that is not a perfect square, $x^2 + bx + c = 0$, you can find a constant d that could be added in to make it a perfect square:

$$x^2 + bx + c + (d - d) = 0; \{\text{Let } b = 2p \text{ and } c + d = p^2\}$$

then:

$$x^2 + 2px + p^2 - d = 0 \text{ and } d = \frac{b^2}{4} - c$$

Once you have completed the square you can find the roots of the resulting equation:

$$x^2 + 2px + p^2 - d = 0$$
$$(x + p)^2 = d$$
$$x + p = \pm\sqrt{d}$$
$$x = -p \pm \sqrt{d}$$

It is worth noting that substituting the original expressions into this solution gives the same result as the quadratic formula where $a = 1$:

$$x = -p \pm \sqrt{d} = -\frac{b}{2} \pm \sqrt{\frac{b^2}{4} - c} = -\frac{b}{2} \pm \frac{\sqrt{b^2 - 4c}}{2} = \frac{-b \pm \sqrt{b^2 - 4c}}{2}$$

Completing the square can be seen as arranging block representations of each of the terms to be as close to a square as possible and then filling in the gaps. For example, consider the quadratic expression $x^2 + 6x + 2$:

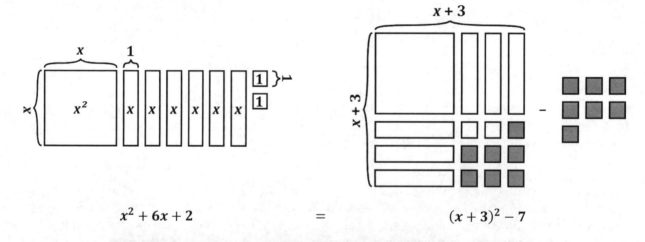

$$x^2 + 6x + 2 \qquad = \qquad (x + 3)^2 - 7$$

> **Review Video: Completing the Square**
> Visit mometrix.com/academy and enter code: 982479

USING GIVEN ROOTS TO FIND QUADRATIC EQUATION

One way to find the roots of a quadratic equation is to factor the equation and use the **zero product property**, setting each factor of the equation equal to zero to find the corresponding root. We can use this technique in reverse to find an equation given its roots. Each root corresponds to a linear equation which in turn corresponds to a factor of the quadratic equation.

For example, we can find a quadratic equation whose roots are $x = 2$ and $x = -1$. The root $x = 2$ corresponds to the equation $x - 2 = 0$, and the root $x = -1$ corresponds to the equation $x + 1 = 0$.

These two equations correspond to the factors $(x - 2)$ and $(x + 1)$, from which we can derive the equation $(x - 2)(x + 1) = 0$, or $x^2 - x - 2 = 0$.

Any integer multiple of this entire equation will also yield the same roots, as the integer will simply cancel out when the equation is factored. For example, $2x^2 - 2x - 4 = 0$ factors as $2(x - 2)(x + 1) = 0$.

Linear Functions and Data Organizations

Algebraic Theorems

According to the **fundamental theorem of algebra**, every non-constant, single-variable polynomial has exactly as many roots as the polynomial's highest exponent. For example, if x^4 is the largest exponent of a term, the polynomial will have exactly 4 roots. However, some of these roots may have multiplicity or be complex numbers. For instance, in the polynomial function $f(x) = x^4 - 4x + 3$, the only real root is 1, though it has multiplicity of 2 – that is, it occurs twice. The other two roots, $(-1 - i\sqrt{2})$ and $(-1 + i\sqrt{2})$, are complex, consisting of both real and non-real components.

The **remainder theorem** is useful for determining the remainder when a polynomial is divided by a binomial. The remainder theorem states that if a polynomial function $f(x)$ is divided by a binomial $x - a$, where a is a real number, the remainder of the division will be the value of $f(a)$. If $f(a) = 0$, then a is a root of the polynomial.

The **factor theorem** is related to the remainder theorem and states that if $f(a) = 0$ then $(x - a)$ is a factor of the function.

According to the **rational root theorem,** any rational root of a polynomial function $f(x) = a_n x^n + a_{n-1} x^{n-1} + \cdots + a_1 x + a_0$ with integer coefficients will, when reduced to its lowest terms, be a positive or negative fraction such that the numerator is a factor of a_0 and the denominator is a factor of a_n. For instance, if the polynomial function $f(x) = x^3 + 3x^2 - 4$ has any rational roots, the numerators of those roots can only be factors of 4 (1, 2, 4), and the denominators can only be factors of 1 (1). The function in this example has roots of 1 (or $\frac{1}{1}$) and –2 (or $\frac{-2}{1}$).

Basic Functions

FUNCTION AND RELATION

When expressing functional relationships, the **variables** x and y are typically used. These values are often written as the **coordinates** (x, y). The x-value is the independent variable and the y-value is the dependent variable. A **relation** is a set of data in which there is not a unique y-value for each x-value in the dataset. This means that there can be two of the same x-values assigned to different y-values. A relation is simply a relationship between the x- and y-values in each coordinate but does not apply to the relationship between the values of x and y in the data set. A **function** is a relation where one quantity depends on the other. For example, the amount of money that you make depends on the number of hours that you work. In a function, each x-value in the data set has one unique y-value because the y-value depends on the x-value.

FUNCTIONS

A function has exactly one value of **output variable** (dependent variable) for each value of the **input variable** (independent variable). The set of all values for the input variable (here assumed to be x) is the domain of the function, and the set of all corresponding values of the output variable (here assumed to be y) is the range of the function. When looking at a graph of an equation, the easiest way to determine if the equation is a function or not is to conduct the vertical line test. If a vertical line drawn through any value of x crosses the graph in more than one place, the equation is not a function.

DETERMINING A FUNCTION

You can determine whether an equation is a **function** by substituting different values into the equation for x. You can display and organize these numbers in a data table. A **data table** contains the values for x and y, which you can also list as coordinates. In order for a function to exist, the table cannot contain any repeating x-values that correspond with different y-values. If each x-coordinate has a unique y-coordinate, the table contains a function. However, there can be repeating y-values that correspond with different x-values. An example of this is when the function contains an exponent. Example: if $x^2 = y$, $2^2 = 4$, and $(-2)^2 = 4$.

> **Review Video: Definition of a Function**
> Visit mometrix.com/academy and enter code: 784611

FINDING THE DOMAIN AND RANGE OF A FUNCTION

The **domain** of a function $f(x)$ is the set of all input values for which the function is defined. The **range** of a function $f(x)$ is the set of all possible output values of the function—that is, of every possible value of $f(x)$, for any value of x in the function's domain. For a function expressed in a table, every input-output pair is given explicitly. To find the domain, we just list all the x-values and to find the range, we just list all the values of $f(x)$. Consider the following example:

x	−1	4	2	1	0	3	8	6
$f(x)$	3	0	3	−1	−1	2	4	6

In this case, the domain would be $\{-1, 4, 2, 1, 0, 3, 8, 6\}$ or, putting them in ascending order, $\{-1, 0, 1, 2, 3, 4, 6, 8\}$. (Putting the values in ascending order isn't strictly necessary, but generally makes the set easier to read.) The range would be $\{3, 0, 3, -1, -1, 2, 4, 6\}$. Note that some of these values appear more than once. This is entirely permissible for a function; while each value of x must be matched to a unique value of $f(x)$, the converse is not true. We don't need to list each value more than once, so eliminating duplicates, the range is $\{3, 0, -1, 2, 4, 6\}$, or, putting them in ascending order, $\{-1, 0, 2, 3, 4, 6\}$.

Note that by definition of a function, no input value can be matched to more than one output value. It is good to double-check to make sure that the data given follows this and is therefore actually a function.

> **Review Video: Domain and Range**
> Visit mometrix.com/academy and enter code: 778133
>
> **Review Video: Domain and Range of Quadratic Functions**
> Visit mometrix.com/academy and enter code: 331768

WRITING A FUNCTION RULE USING A TABLE

If given a set of data, place the corresponding x- and y-values into a table and analyze the relationship between them. Consider what you can do to each x-value to obtain the corresponding y-value. Try adding or subtracting different numbers to and from x and then try multiplying or dividing different numbers to and from x. If none of these **operations** give you the y-value, try combining the operations. Once you find a rule that works for one pair, make sure to try it with each additional set of ordered pairs in the table. If the same operation or combination of operations satisfies each set of coordinates, then the table contains a function. The rule is then used to write the equation of the function in "$y = f(x)$" form.

DIRECT AND INVERSE VARIATIONS OF VARIABLES

Variables that vary directly are those that either both increase at the same rate or both decrease at the same rate. For example, in the functions $y = kx$ or $y = kx^n$, where k and n are positive, the value of y increases as the value of x increases and decreases as the value of x decreases.

Variables that vary inversely are those where one increases while the other decreases. For example, in the functions $y = \frac{k}{x}$ or $y = \frac{k}{x^n}$ where k and n are positive, the value of y increases as the value of x decreases and decreases as the value of x increases.

In both cases, k is the constant of variation.

PROPERTIES OF FUNCTIONS

There are many different ways to classify functions based on their structure or behavior. Important features of functions include:

- **End behavior**: the behavior of the function at extreme values ($f(x)$ as $x \to \pm\infty$)
- **y-intercept**: the value of the function at $f(0)$
- **Roots**: the values of x where the function equals zero ($f(x) = 0$)
- **Extrema**: minimum or maximum values of the function or where the function changes direction ($f(x) \geq k$ or $f(x) \leq k$)

CLASSIFICATION OF FUNCTIONS

An **invertible function** is defined as a function, $f(x)$, for which there is another function, $f^{-1}(x)$, such that $f^{-1}(f(x)) = x$. For example, if $f(x) = 3x - 2$ the inverse function, $f^{-1}(x)$, can be found:

$$x = 3(f^{-1}(x)) - 2$$
$$\frac{x+2}{3} = f^{-1}(x)$$

$$f^{-1}(f(x)) = \frac{3x - 2 + 2}{3}$$
$$= \frac{3x}{3}$$
$$= x$$

Note that $f^{-1}(x)$ is a valid function over all values of x.

In a **one-to-one function**, each value of x has exactly one value for y on the coordinate plane (this is the definition of a function) and each value of y has exactly one value for x. While the vertical line test will determine if a graph is that of a function, the horizontal line test will determine if a function is a one-to-one function. If a horizontal line drawn at any value of y intersects the graph in more than one place, the graph is not that of a one-to-one function. Do not make the mistake of using the horizontal line test exclusively in determining if a graph is that of a one-to-one function. A one-to-one function must pass both the vertical line test and the horizontal line test. As such, one-to-one functions are invertible functions.

A **many-to-one function** is a function whereby the relation is a function, but the inverse of the function is not a function. In other words, each element in the domain is mapped to one and only one element in the range. However, one or more elements in the range may be mapped to the same element in the domain. A graph of a many-to-one function would pass the vertical line test, but not the horizontal line test. This is why many-to-one functions are not invertible.

A **monotone function** is a function whose graph either constantly increases or constantly decreases. Examples include the functions $f(x) = x$, $f(x) = -x$, or $f(x) = x^3$.

An **even function** has a graph that is symmetric with respect to the y-axis and satisfies the equation $f(x) = f(-x)$. Examples include the functions $f(x) = x^2$ and $f(x) = ax^n$, where a is any real number and n is a positive even integer.

An **odd function** has a graph that is symmetric with respect to the origin and satisfies the equation $f(x) = -f(-x)$. Examples include the functions $f(x) = x^3$ and $f(x) = ax^n$, where a is any real number and n is a positive odd integer.

> **Review Video: Even and Odd Functions**
> Visit mometrix.com/academy and enter code: 278985

Constant functions are given by the equation $f(x) = b$, where b is a real number. There is no independent variable present in the equation, so the function has a constant value for all x. The graph of a constant function is a horizontal line of slope 0 that is positioned b units from the x-axis. If b is positive, the line is above the x-axis; if b is negative, the line is below the x-axis.

Identity functions are identified by the equation $f(x) = x$, where every value of the function is equal to its corresponding value of x. The only zero is the point (0,0). The graph is a line with a slope of 1.

In **linear functions**, the value of the function changes in direct proportion to x. The rate of change, represented by the slope on its graph, is constant throughout. The standard form of a linear equation is $ax + cy = d$, where a, c, and d are real numbers. As a function, this equation is commonly in the form $y = mx + b$ or $f(x) = mx + b$ where $m = -\frac{a}{c}$ and $b = \frac{d}{c}$. This is known as the slope-intercept form, because the coefficients give the slope of the graphed function (m) and its y-intercept (b). Solve the equation $mx + b = 0$ for x to get $x = -\frac{b}{m}$, which is the only zero of the function. The domain and range are both the set of all real numbers.

> **Review Video: Graphing Linear Functions**
> Visit mometrix.com/academy and enter code: 699478

Algebraic functions are those that exclusively use polynomials and roots. These would include polynomial functions, rational functions, square root functions, and all combinations of these functions, such as polynomials as the radicand. These combinations may be joined by addition, subtraction, multiplication, or division, but may not include variables as exponents.

> **Review Video: Common Functions**
> Visit mometrix.com/academy and enter code: 629798

ABSOLUTE VALUE FUNCTIONS

An **absolute value function** is in the format $f(x) = |ax + b|$. Like other functions, the domain is the set of all real numbers. However, because absolute value indicates positive numbers, the range is limited to positive real numbers. To find the zero of an absolute value function, set the portion inside the absolute value sign equal to zero and solve for x. An absolute value function is also known as a piecewise function because it must be solved in pieces—one for if the value inside the absolute value sign is positive, and one for if the value is negative. The function can be expressed as:

$$f(x) = \begin{cases} ax + b & \text{if } ax + b \geq 0 \\ -(ax + b) & \text{if } ax + b < 0 \end{cases}$$

This will allow for an accurate statement of the range. The graph of an example absolute value function, $f(x) = |2x - 1|$, is below:

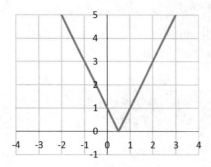

PIECEWISE FUNCTIONS

A **piecewise function** is a function that has different definitions on two or more different intervals. The following, for instance, is one example of a piecewise-defined function:

$$f(x) = \begin{cases} x^2, & x < 0 \\ x, & 0 \le x \le 2 \\ (x-2)^2, & x > 2 \end{cases}$$

To graph this function, you would simply graph each part separately in the appropriate domain. The final graph would look like this:

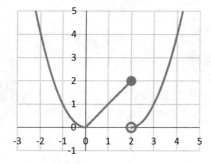

Note the filled and hollow dots at the discontinuity at $x = 2$. This is important to show which side of the graph that point corresponds to. Because $f(x) = x$ on the closed interval $0 \le x \le 2$, $f(2) = 2$. The point $(2, 2)$ is therefore marked with a filled circle, and the point $(2,0)$, which is the endpoint of the rightmost $(x - 2)^2$ part of the graph but *not actually part of the function*, is marked with a hollow dot to indicate this.

> **Review Video: Piecewise Functions**
> Visit mometrix.com/academy and enter code: 707921

QUADRATIC FUNCTIONS

A **quadratic function** is a function in the form $y = ax^2 + bx + c$, where a does not equal 0. While a linear function forms a line, a quadratic function forms a **parabola**, which is a u-shaped figure that either opens upward or downward. A parabola that opens upward is said to be a **positive quadratic function,** and a parabola that opens downward is said to be a **negative quadratic function**. The shape of a parabola can differ, depending on the values of a, b, and c. All parabolas contain a **vertex**, which is the highest possible point, the **maximum**, or the lowest possible point, the **minimum**. This is the point where the graph begins moving in the opposite direction. A

56

quadratic function can have zero, one, or two solutions, and therefore zero, one, or two x-intercepts. Recall that the x-intercepts are referred to as the zeros, or roots, of a function. A quadratic function will have only one y-intercept. Understanding the basic components of a quadratic function can give you an idea of the shape of its graph.

Example graph of a positive quadratic function, $x^2 + 2x - 3$:

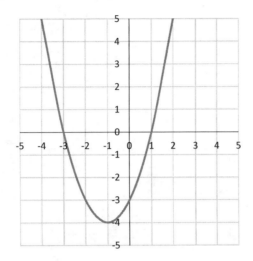

POLYNOMIAL FUNCTIONS

A **polynomial function** is a function with multiple terms and multiple powers of x, such as:

$$f(x) = a_n x^n + a_{n-1} x^{n-1} + a_{n-2} x^{n-2} + \cdots + a_1 x + a_0$$

where n is a non-negative integer that is the highest exponent in the polynomial and $a_n \neq 0$. The domain of a polynomial function is the set of all real numbers. If the greatest exponent in the polynomial is even, the polynomial is said to be of even degree and the range is the set of real numbers that satisfy the function. If the greatest exponent in the polynomial is odd, the polynomial is said to be odd and the range, like the domain, is the set of all real numbers.

RATIONAL FUNCTIONS

A **rational function** is a function that can be constructed as a ratio of two polynomial expressions: $f(x) = \frac{p(x)}{q(x)}$, where $p(x)$ and $q(x)$ are both polynomial expressions and $q(x) \neq 0$. The domain is the set of all real numbers, except any values for which $q(x) = 0$. The range is the set of real numbers that satisfies the function when the domain is applied. When you graph a rational function, you will have vertical asymptotes wherever $q(x) = 0$. If the polynomial in the numerator is of lesser degree than the polynomial in the denominator, the x-axis will also be a horizontal asymptote. If the numerator and denominator have equal degrees, there will be a horizontal asymptote not on the x-axis. If the degree of the numerator is exactly one greater than the degree of the denominator, the graph will have an oblique, or diagonal, asymptote. The asymptote will be along the line $y = \frac{p_n}{q_{n-1}} x + \frac{p_{n-1}}{q_{n-1}}$, where p_n and q_{n-1} are the coefficients of the highest degree terms in their respective polynomials.

SQUARE ROOT FUNCTIONS

A **square root function** is a function that contains a radical and is in the format $f(x) = \sqrt{ax + b}$. The domain is the set of all real numbers that yields a positive radicand or a radicand equal to zero.

Because square root values are assumed to be positive unless otherwise identified, the range is all real numbers from zero to infinity. To find the zero of a square root function, set the radicand equal to zero and solve for x. The graph of a square root function is always to the right of the zero and always above the x-axis.

Example graph of a square root function, $f(x) = \sqrt{2x+1}$:

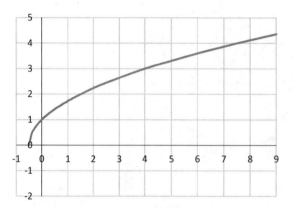

Working with Functions

MANIPULATION OF FUNCTIONS

Translation occurs when values are added to or subtracted from the x- or y-values. If a constant is added to the y-portion of each point, the graph shifts up. If a constant is subtracted from the y-portion of each point, the graph shifts down. This is represented by the expression $f(x) \pm k$, where k is a constant. If a constant is added to the x-portion of each point, the graph shifts left. If a constant is subtracted from the x-portion of each point, the graph shifts right. This is represented by the expression $f(x \pm k)$, where k is a constant.

Stretching, compression, and reflection occur when different parts of a function are multiplied by different groups of constants. If the function as a whole is multiplied by a real number constant greater than 1, $(k \times f(x))$, the graph is stretched vertically. If k in the previous equation is greater than zero but less than 1, the graph is compressed vertically. If k is less than zero, the graph is reflected about the x-axis, in addition to being either stretched or compressed vertically if k is less than or greater than –1, respectively. If instead, just the x-term is multiplied by a constant greater than 1 $(f(k \times x))$, the graph is compressed horizontally. If k in the previous equation is greater than zero but less than 1, the graph is stretched horizontally. If k is less than zero, the graph is reflected about the y-axis, in addition to being either stretched or compressed horizontally if k is greater than or less than –1, respectively.

> **Review Video: <u>Manipulation of Functions</u>**
> Visit mometrix.com/academy and enter code: 669117

APPLYING THE BASIC OPERATIONS TO FUNCTIONS

For each of the basic operations, we will use these functions as examples: $f(x) = x^2$ and $g(x) = x$.

To find the sum of two functions f and g, assuming the domains are compatible, simply add the two functions together: $(f + g)(x) = f(x) + g(x) = x^2 + x$.

To find the difference of two functions f and g, assuming the domains are compatible, simply subtract the second function from the first: $(f - g)(x) = f(x) - g(x) = x^2 - x$.

To find the product of two functions f and g, assuming the domains are compatible, multiply the two functions together: $(f \times g)(x) = f(x) \times g(x) = x^2 \times x = x^3$.

To find the quotient of two functions f and g, assuming the domains are compatible, divide the first function by the second: $\frac{f}{g}(x) = \frac{f(x)}{g(x)} = \frac{x^2}{x} = x \,; x \neq 0$.

The example given in each case is fairly simple, but on a given problem, if you are looking only for the value of the sum, difference, product, or quotient of two functions at a particular x-value, it may be simpler to solve the functions individually and then perform the given operation using those values.

The composite of two functions f and g, written as $(f \circ g)(x)$ simply means that the output of the second function is used as the input of the first. This can also be written as $f(g(x))$. In general, this can be solved by substituting $g(x)$ for all instances of x in $f(x)$ and simplifying. Using the example functions $f(x) = x^2 - x + 2$ and $g(x) = x + 1$, we can find that $(f \circ g)(x)$ or $f(g(x))$ is equal to $f(x + 1) = (x + 1)^2 - (x + 1) + 2$, which simplifies to $x^2 + x + 2$.

It is important to note that $(f \circ g)(x)$ is not necessarily the same as $(g \circ f)(x)$. The process is not always commutative like addition or multiplication expressions. It *can* be commutative, but most often this is not the case.

EVALUATING LINEAR FUNCTIONS

A **function** can be expressed as an equation that relates an input to an output where each input corresponds to exactly one output. The input of a function is defined by the x-variable, and the output is defined by the y-variable. For example, consider the function $y = 2x + 6$. The value of y, the output, is determined by the value of the x, the input. If the value of x is 3, the value of y is $y = 2(3) + 6 = 6 + 6 = 12$. This means that when $x = 3$, $y = 12$. This can be expressed as the ordered pair (3,12).

It is common for function equations to use the form $f(x) =$ instead of $y =$. However, $f(x)$ and y represent the same thing. We read $f(x)$ as "f of x." "f of x" implies that the value of f depends on the value of x. The function used in the example above could be expressed as $y = 2x + 6$ or $f(x) = 2x + 6$. Both functions represent the same line when graphed.

Functions that are expressed in the form $f(x) =$ are evaluated in the same way the equations are evaluated in the form $y =$. For example, when evaluating the function $f(x) = 3x - 2$ for $f(6)$, substitute 6 in for x, and simplify. $f(x) = 3x - 2$ becomes $f(6) = 3(6) - 2 = 18 - 2 = 16$. When x is 6, $f(x)$ is 16.

Find the value of $f(8)$.

$$f(x) = 3x - 2$$
$$f(8) = 3(8) - 2$$
$$f(8) = 22$$

Advanced Functions

STEP FUNCTIONS

The double brackets indicate a step function. For a step function, the value inside the double brackets is rounded down to the nearest integer. The graph of the function $f_0(x) = [\![x]\!]$ appears on the left graph. In comparison $f(x) = 2\left[\!\left[\frac{1}{3}(x-1)\right]\!\right]$ is on the right graph. The coefficient of 2 shows that it's stretched vertically by a factor of 2 (so there's a vertical distance of 2 units between successive "steps"). The coefficient of $\frac{1}{3}$ in front of the x shows that it's stretched horizontally by a factor of 3 (so each "step" is three units long), and the $x-1$ shows that it's displaced one unit to the right.

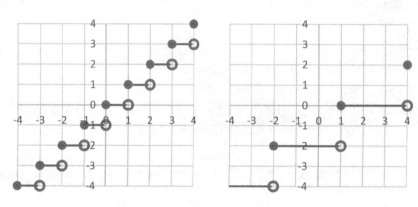

TRANSCENDENTAL FUNCTIONS

Transcendental functions are all functions that are non-algebraic. Any function that includes logarithms, trigonometric functions, variables as exponents, or any combination that includes any of these is not algebraic in nature, even if the function includes polynomials or roots.

EXPONENTIAL FUNCTIONS

Exponential functions are equations that have the format $y = b^x$, where base $b > 0$ and $b \neq 1$. The exponential function can also be written $f(x) = b^x$. Recall the properties of exponents, like the product of terms with the same base is equal to the base raised to the sum of the exponents $(a^x \times a^y = a^{x+y})$ and a term with an exponent that is raised to an exponent is equal to the base of the original term raised to the product of the exponents: $((a^x)^y = a^{xy})$. The graph of an example exponential function, $f(x) = 2^x$, is below:

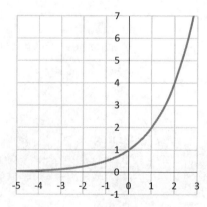

60

Note in the graph that the y-value approaches zero to the left and infinity to the right. One of the key features of an exponential function is that there will be one end that goes off to infinity and another that asymptotically approaches a lower bound. Common forms of exponential functions include:

Geometric sequences: $a_n = a_1 \times r^{n-1}$, where a_n is the value of the nth term, a_1 is the initial value, r is the common ratio, and n is the number of terms. Note that $a_1 \times r^{1-1} = a_1 \times r^0 = a_1 \times 1 = a_1$.

Population growth: $f(t) = ae^{rt}$, where $f(t)$ is the population at time $t \geq 0$, a is the initial population, e is the mathematical constant known as Euler's number, and r is the growth rate.

> **Review Video: Population Growth**
> Visit mometrix.com/academy and enter code: 109278

Compound interest: $f(t) = P\left(1 + \frac{r}{n}\right)^{nt}$, where $f(t)$ is the account value at a certain number of time periods $t \geq 0$, P is the initial principal balance, r is the interest rate, and n is the number of times the interest is applied per time period.

> **Review Video: Interest Functions**
> Visit mometrix.com/academy and enter code: 559176

General exponential growth or decay: $f(t) = a(1 + r)^t$, where $f(t)$ is the future count, a is the current or initial count, r is the growth or decay rate, and t is the time.

For example, suppose the initial population of a town was 1,200 people. The annual population growth is 5%. The current population is 2,400. To find out how much time has passed since the town was founded, we can use the following function:

$$2,400 = 1,200e^{0.05t}.$$

The general form for population growth may be represented as $f(t) = ae^{rt}$, where $f(t)$ represents the current population, a represents the initial population, r represents the growth rate, and t represents the time. Thus, substituting the initial population, current population, and rate into this form gives the equation above.

The number of years that have passed were found by first dividing both sides of the equation by 1,200. Doing so gives $2 = e^{0.05t}$. Taking the natural logarithm of both sides gives $\ln(2) = ln(e^{0.05t})$. Applying the power property of logarithms, the equation may be rewritten as $\ln(2) = 0.05t \times \ln(e)$, which simplifies as $\ln(2) = 0.05t$. Dividing both sides of this equation by 0.05 gives $t \approx 13.86$. Thus, approximately 13.86 years passed.

LOGARITHMIC FUNCTIONS

Logarithmic functions are equations that have the format $y = \log_b x$ or $f(x) = \log_b x$. The base b may be any number except one; however, the most common bases for logarithms are base 10 and base e. The log base e is the natural logarithm, or ln, expressed by the function $f(x) = \ln x$.

Any logarithm that does not have an assigned value of b is assumed to be base 10: $\log x = \log_{10} x$. Exponential functions and logarithmic functions are related in that one is the inverse of the other. If $f(x) = b^x$, then $f^{-1}(x) = \log_b x$. This can perhaps be expressed more clearly by the two equations: $y = b^x$ and $x = \log_b y$.

The following properties apply to logarithmic expressions:

Property	Description
$\log_b 1 = 0$	The log of 1 is equal to 0 for any base
$\log_b b = 1$	The log of the base is equal to 1
$\log_b b^p = p$	The log of the base raised to a power is equal to that power
$\log_b MN = \log_b M + \log_b N$	The log of a product is the sum of the log of each factor
$\log_b \dfrac{M}{N} = \log_b M - \log_b N$	The log of a quotient is equal to the log of the dividend minus the log of the divisor
$\log_b M^p = p \log_b M$	The log of a value raised to a power is equal to the power times the log of the value

The graph of an example logarithmic function, $f(x) = \log_2(x + 2)$, is below:

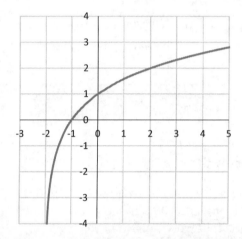

Review Video: Logarithmic Function
Visit mometrix.com/academy and enter code: 658985

TRIGONOMETRIC FUNCTIONS

Trigonometric functions are periodic, meaning that they repeat the same form over and over. The basic trigonometric functions are sine (abbreviated 'sin'), cosine (abbreviated 'cos'), and tangent (abbreviated 'tan'). The simplest way to think of them is as describing the ratio of the side lengths of a right triangle in relation to the angles of the triangle.

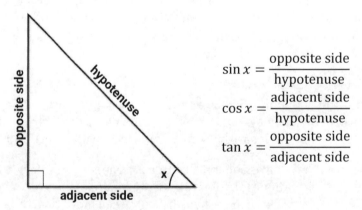

$$\sin x = \frac{\text{opposite side}}{\text{hypotenuse}}$$

$$\cos x = \frac{\text{adjacent side}}{\text{hypotenuse}}$$

$$\tan x = \frac{\text{opposite side}}{\text{adjacent side}}$$

Using sine as an example, trigonometric functions take the form $f(x) = A \sin(Bx + C) + D$, where the **amplitude** is simply equal to A. The **period** is the distance between successive peaks or troughs, essentially the length of the repeated pattern. In this form, the period is equal to $\frac{2\pi}{B}$. As for C, this is the **phase shift** or the horizontal shift of the function. The last term, D, is the vertical shift and determines the **midline** as $y = D$.

For instance, consider the function $f(x) = 2 + \frac{3}{2}\sin\left(\pi x + \frac{\pi}{2}\right)$. Here, $A = \frac{3}{2}$, $B = \pi$, $C = \frac{\pi}{2}$, and $D = 2$, so the midline is at $y = 2$, the amplitude is $\frac{3}{2}$, and the period is $\frac{2\pi}{\pi} = 2$. To graph this function, we center the sine wave on the midline and extend it to a height above and below the midline equal to the amplitude—so this graph would have a minimum value of $2 - \frac{3}{2} = \frac{1}{2}$ and a maximum of $2 + \frac{3}{2} = \frac{7}{2}$. So, the function would be graphed as follows:

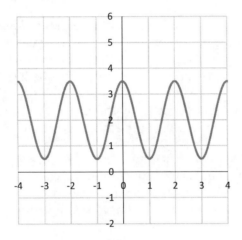

Sequences

A **sequence** is an ordered set of numbers that continues in a defined pattern. The function that defines a sequence has a domain composed of the set of positive integers. Each member of the sequence is an element, or individual term. Each element is identified by the notation a_n, where a is the term of the sequence, and n is the integer identifying which term in the sequence a is.

There are two different ways to represent a sequence that contains the element a_n. The first is the simple notation $\{a_n\}$. The second is the expanded notation of a sequence: $a_1, a_2, a_3, \ldots a_n, \ldots$. Notice that the expanded form does not end with the nth term. There is no indication that the nth term is the last term in the sequence, only that the nth term is an element of the sequence.

ARITHMETIC SEQUENCES

An **arithmetic sequence**, or arithmetic progression, is a special kind of sequence in which a specific quantity, called the common difference, is added to each term to make the next term. The common difference may be positive or negative. The general form of an arithmetic sequence containing n terms is $a_1, a_1 + d, a_1 + 2d, \ldots, a_1 + (n - 1)d$, where d is the common difference. The general formula for any term of an arithmetic sequence is $a_n = a_1 + (n - 1)d$, where a_n is the term you are looking for and d is the common difference. To find the sum of the first n terms of an arithmetic sequence, use the formula $s_n = \frac{n}{2}(a_1 + a_n)$.

MONOTONIC SEQUENCES

A **monotonic sequence** is a sequence that is either nonincreasing or nondecreasing. A **nonincreasing** sequence is one whose terms either get progressively smaller in value or remain the same. Such a sequence is always bounded above, that is, all elements of the sequence must be less than some real number. A **nondecreasing** sequence is one whose terms either get progressively larger in value or remain the same. Such a sequence is always bounded below, that is, all elements of the sequence must be greater than some real number.

RECURSIVE SEQUENCES

When one element of a sequence is defined in terms of a previous element or elements of the sequence, the sequence is a **recursive sequence**. For example, given the recursive definition $a_1 = 1; a_2 = 1; a_n = a_{n-1} + a_{n-2}$ for all $n > 2$, you get the sequence 1,1,2,3,5,8, ... This is known as the Fibonacci sequence: a continuing sequence of numbers in which each number (after a_2) is the sum of the two previous numbers. The Fibonacci sequence can be defined as starting with either 1,1 or 0,1. Both definitions are considered correct in mathematics. Make sure you know which definition you are working with when dealing with Fibonacci numbers.

Sometimes in a recursive sequence, the terms can be found using a general formula that does not involve the previous terms of the sequence. Such a formula is called a **closed-form** expression for a recursive definition—an alternate formula that will generate the same sequence of numbers. However, not all sequences based on recursive definitions will have a closed-form expression. Some sequences will require the use of the recursive definition.

THE GOLDEN RATIO AND THE FIBONACCI SEQUENCE

The golden ratio is approximately 1.6180339887 and is often represented by the Greek letter phi, Φ. The exact value of Φ is $\frac{(1+\sqrt{5})}{2}$ and it is one of the solutions to $x - \frac{1}{x} = 1$. The golden ratio can be found using the Fibonacci sequence, since the ratio of a term to the previous term approaches Φ as the sequence approaches infinity:

n	a_n	a_{n-1}	$\dfrac{a_n}{a_{n-1}}$
3	2	1	2
4	3	2	1.5
5	5	3	$1.\overline{6}$
6	8	5	1.6
7	13	8	1.625
8	21	13	$1.\overline{615384}$
9	34	21	$1.\overline{619047}$
⋮	⋮	⋮	⋮
20	6,765	4,181	1.618033963 ...

GEOMETRIC SEQUENCES

A geometric sequence is a sequence in which each term is multiplied by a constant number (called the common ratio) to get the next term. Essentially, it's the same concept as an arithmetic sequence, but with multiplication instead of addition.

Consider the following example of a geometric sequence: Andy opens a savings account with $10. During each subsequent week, he plans to double the amount from the previous week.

Sequence: $10, 20, 40, 80, 160, \dots$

Function: $a_n = 10 \times 2^{n-1}$

This is a geometric sequence with a common ratio of 2. All geometric sequences represent exponential functions. The nth term in any geometric sequence is $a_n = a_1 \times r^{n-1}$, where a_n represents the value of the nth term, a_1 is the initial term, r is the common ratio, and n is the number of terms. Thus, substituting the initial value of 10 and common ratio of 2 gives the function $a_n = 10 \times 2^{n-1}$.

> **Review Video: Geometric Sequences**
> Visit mometrix.com/academy and enter code: 140779

Advanced Sequences and Series

LIMIT OF A SEQUENCE

Some sequences will have a **limit**—a value the sequence approaches, or sometimes even reaches, but never passes. A sequence with a limit is called a **convergent** sequence because all the values of the sequence seemingly converge at that point. Sequences that do not converge at a particular limit are **divergent** sequences. The easiest way to determine whether a sequence converges or diverges is to find the limit of the sequence. If the limit is a real number, the sequence is convergent. If the limit is infinity, the sequence is divergent.

Remember the following rules for finding limits:

- $\lim_{n \to \infty} k = k$, for all real numbers k
- $\lim_{n \to \infty} \frac{1}{n} = 0$
- $\lim_{n \to \infty} n = \infty$
- $\lim_{n \to \infty} \frac{k}{n^p} = 0$, for all real numbers k and positive rational numbers p
- The limit of the sum of two sequences is equal to the sum of the limits of the two sequences: $\lim_{n \to \infty} (a_n + b_n) = \lim_{n \to \infty} a_n + \lim_{n \to \infty} b_n$
- The limit of the difference between two sequences is equal to the difference between the limits of the two sequences: $\lim_{n \to \infty} (a_n - b_n) = \lim_{n \to \infty} a_n - \lim_{n \to \infty} b_n$
- The limit of the product of two sequences is equal to the product of the limits of the two sequences: $\lim_{n \to \infty} (a_n \times b_n) = \lim_{n \to \infty} a_n \times \lim_{n \to \infty} b_n$

- The limit of the quotient of two sequences is equal to the quotient of the limits of the two sequences, with some exceptions: $\lim_{n\to\infty}\left(\frac{a_n}{b_n}\right) = \frac{\lim_{n\to\infty} a_n}{\lim_{n\to\infty} b_n}$. In the quotient formula, it is important that $b_n \neq 0$ and that $\lim_{n\to\infty} b_n \neq 0$.

- The limit of a sequence multiplied by a scalar is equal to the scalar multiplied by the limit of the sequence: $\lim_{n\to\infty} ka_n = k \lim_{n\to\infty} a_n$, where k is any real number

> **Review Video: Limit of a Sequence**
> Visit mometrix.com/academy and enter code: 847732

INFINITE SERIES

Both arithmetic and geometric sequences have formulas to find the sum of the first n terms in the sequence, assuming you know what the first term is. The sum of all the terms in a sequence is called a series. An **infinite series** is an infinite sum. In other words, it is what you get by adding up all the terms in an infinite sequence: $\sum_{n=1}^{\infty} a_n = a_1 + a_2 + a_3 + \cdots + a_n + \cdots$. This notation can be shortened to $\sum_{n=1}^{\infty} a_n$ or $\sum a_n$.

While we can't add up an infinite list of numbers one at a time, we can still determine the infinite sum. As we add the terms in a series, we can imagine an infinite sequence of partial sums, where the first partial sum is the first element of the series, the second partial sum is the sum of the first two elements of the series, and the nth partial sum is the sum of the first n elements of the series.

Every infinite sequence of partial sums (infinite series) either converges or diverges. As with the test for convergence in a sequence, finding the limit of the sequence of partial sums will indicate whether it is a converging series or a diverging series. If there exists a real number S such that $\lim_{n\to\infty} S_n = S$, where S_n is the sequence of partial sums, then the series converges. If the limit equals infinity, then the series diverges. If $\lim_{n\to\infty} S_n = S$ and S is a real number, then S is also the convergence value of the series.

To find the sum as n approaches infinity for the sum of two convergent series, find the sum as n approaches infinity for each individual series and add the results.

$$\sum_{n=1}^{\infty} (a_n + b_n) = \sum_{n=1}^{\infty} a_n + \sum_{n=1}^{\infty} b_n$$

The same idea works for subtraction.

$$\sum_{n=1}^{\infty} (a_n - b_n) = \sum_{n=1}^{\infty} a_n - \sum_{n=1}^{\infty} b_n$$

66

To find the sum as n approaches infinity for the product of a constant (also called a scalar) and a convergent series, find the sum as n approaches infinity for the series and multiply the result by the scalar.

$$\sum_{n=1}^{\infty} k a_n = k \sum_{n=1}^{\infty} a_n$$

The nth **term test for divergence** means taking the limit of a sequence a_n as n goes to infinity $\left(\lim_{n\to\infty} a_n\right)$ and checking whether the limit is zero. If the limit is not zero, then the series $\sum a_n$ is a diverging series. This test only works to prove divergence, however. If the limit is zero, the test is inconclusive, meaning the series could be either convergent or divergent.

Probability

Probability is the likelihood of a certain outcome occurring for a given event. An **event** is any situation that produces a result. It could be something as simple as flipping a coin or as complex as launching a rocket. Determining the probability of an outcome for an event can be equally simple or complex. As such, there are specific terms used in the study of probability that need to be understood:

- **Compound event**—an event that involves two or more independent events (rolling a pair of dice and taking the sum)
- **Desired outcome** (or success)—an outcome that meets a particular set of criteria (a roll of 1 or 2 if we are looking for numbers less than 3)
- **Independent events**—two or more events whose outcomes do not affect one another (two coins tossed at the same time)
- **Dependent events**—two or more events whose outcomes affect one another (two cards drawn consecutively from the same deck)
- **Certain outcome**—probability of outcome is 100% or 1
- **Impossible outcome**—probability of outcome is 0% or 0
- **Mutually exclusive outcomes**—two or more outcomes whose criteria cannot all be satisfied in a single event (a coin coming up heads and tails on the same toss)
- **Random variable**—refers to all possible outcomes of a single event which may be discrete or continuous.

SAMPLE SPACE

The total set of all possible results of a test or experiment is called a **sample space**, or sometimes a universal sample space. The sample space, represented by one of the variables S, Ω, or U (for universal sample space) has individual elements called outcomes. Other terms for outcome that may be used interchangeably include elementary outcome, simple event, or sample point. The number of outcomes in a given sample space could be infinite or finite, and some tests may yield multiple unique sample sets. For example, tests conducted by drawing playing cards from a standard deck would have one sample space of the card values, another sample space of the card suits, and a third sample space of suit-denomination combinations. For most tests, the sample spaces considered will be finite.

An **event**, represented by the variable E, is a portion of a sample space. It may be one outcome or a group of outcomes from the same sample space. If an event occurs, then the test or experiment will generate an outcome that satisfies the requirement of that event. For example, given a standard deck of 52 playing cards as the sample space, and defining the event as the collection of face cards, then the event will occur if the card drawn is a J, Q, or K. If any other card is drawn, the event is said to have not occurred.

For every sample space, each possible outcome has a specific likelihood, or probability, that it will occur. The probability measure, also called the **distribution**, is a function that assigns a real number probability, from zero to one, to each outcome. For a probability measure to be accurate, every outcome must have a real number probability measure that is greater than or equal to zero and less than or equal to one. Also, the probability measure of the sample space must equal one, and the probability measure of the union of multiple outcomes must equal the sum of the individual probability measures.

Probabilities of events are expressed as real numbers from zero to one. They give a numerical value to the chance that a particular event will occur. The probability of an event occurring is the sum of the probabilities of the individual elements of that event. For example, in a standard deck of 52 playing cards as the sample space and the collection of face cards as the event, the probability of drawing a specific face card is $\frac{1}{52} = 0.019$, but the probability of drawing any one of the twelve face cards is $12(0.019) = 0.228$. Note that rounding of numbers can generate different results. If you multiplied 12 by the fraction $\frac{1}{52}$ before converting to a decimal, you would get the answer $\frac{12}{52} = 0.231$.

THEORETICAL AND EXPERIMENTAL PROBABILITY

Theoretical probability can usually be determined without actually performing the event. The likelihood of an outcome occurring, or the probability of an outcome occurring, is given by the formula:

$$P(A) = \frac{\text{Number of acceptable outcomes}}{\text{Number of possible outcomes}}$$

Note that $P(A)$ is the probability of an outcome A occurring, and each outcome is just as likely to occur as any other outcome. If each outcome has the same probability of occurring as every other possible outcome, the outcomes are said to be equally likely to occur. The total number of acceptable outcomes must be less than or equal to the total number of possible outcomes. If the two are equal, then the outcome is certain to occur and the probability is 1. If the number of acceptable outcomes is zero, then the outcome is impossible and the probability is 0. For example, if there are 20 marbles in a bag and 5 are red, then the theoretical probability of randomly selecting a red marble is 5 out of 20, $\left(\frac{5}{20} = \frac{1}{4}, 0.25, \text{ or } 25\%\right)$.

If the theoretical probability is unknown or too complicated to calculate, it can be estimated by an experimental probability. **Experimental probability**, also called empirical probability, is an estimate of the likelihood of a certain outcome based on repeated experiments or collected data. In other words, while theoretical probability is based on what *should* happen, experimental probability is based on what *has* happened. Experimental probability is calculated in the same way as theoretical probability, except that actual outcomes are used instead of possible outcomes. The more experiments performed or datapoints gathered, the better the estimate should be.

Theoretical and experimental probability do not always line up with one another. Theoretical probability says that out of 20 coin-tosses, 10 should be heads. However, if we were actually to toss 20 coins, we might record just 5 heads. This doesn't mean that our theoretical probability is incorrect; it just means that this particular experiment had results that were different from what was predicted. A practical application of empirical probability is the insurance industry. There are no set functions that define lifespan, health, or safety. Insurance companies look at factors from hundreds of thousands of individuals to find patterns that they then use to set the formulas for insurance premiums.

> **Review Video: Empirical Probability**
> Visit mometrix.com/academy and enter code: 513468

OBJECTIVE AND SUBJECTIVE PROBABILITY

Objective probability is based on mathematical formulas and documented evidence. Examples of objective probability include raffles or lottery drawings where there is a pre-determined number of possible outcomes and a predetermined number of outcomes that correspond to an event. Other cases of objective probability include probabilities of rolling dice, flipping coins, or drawing cards. Most gambling games are based on objective probability.

In contrast, **subjective probability** is based on personal or professional feelings and judgments. Often, there is a lot of guesswork following extensive research. Areas where subjective probability is applicable include sales trends and business expenses. Attractions set admission prices based on subjective probabilities of attendance based on varying admission rates in an effort to maximize their profit.

COMPLEMENT OF AN EVENT

Sometimes it may be easier to calculate the possibility of something not happening, or the **complement of an event**. Represented by the symbol $\bar{A}$, the complement of A is the probability that event A does not happen. When you know the probability of event A occurring, you can use the formula $P(\bar{A}) = 1 - P(A)$, where $P(\bar{A})$ is the probability of event A not occurring, and $P(A)$ is the probability of event A occurring.

ADDITION RULE

The **addition rule** for probability is used for finding the probability of a compound event. Use the formula $P(A \cup B) = P(A) + P(B) - P(A \cap B)$, where $P(A \cap B)$ is the probability of both events occurring to find the probability of a compound event. The probability of both events occurring at the same time must be subtracted to eliminate any overlap in the first two probabilities.

CONDITIONAL PROBABILITY

Given two events A and B, the **conditional probability** $P(A|B)$ is the probability that event A will occur, given that event B has occurred. The conditional probability cannot be calculated simply from $P(A)$ and $P(B)$; these probabilities alone do not give sufficient information to determine the conditional probability. It can, however, be determined if you are also given the probability of the intersection of events A and B, $P(A \cap B)$, the probability that events A and B both occur.

Specifically, $P(A|B) = \frac{P(A \cap B)}{P(B)}$. For instance, suppose you have a jar containing two red marbles and two blue marbles, and you draw two marbles at random. Consider event A being the event that the first marble drawn is red, and event B being the event that the second marble drawn is blue. If we want to find the probability that B occurs given that A occurred, $P(B|A)$, then we can compute it using the fact that $P(A)$ is $\frac{1}{2}$, and $P(A \cap B)$ is $\frac{1}{3}$. (The latter may not be obvious, but may be determined by finding the product of $\frac{1}{2}$ and $\frac{2}{3}$). Therefore $P(B|A) = \frac{P(A \cap B)}{P(A)} = \frac{1/3}{1/2} = \frac{2}{3}$.

CONDITIONAL PROBABILITY IN EVERYDAY SITUATIONS

Conditional probability often arises in everyday situations in, for example, estimating the risk or benefit of certain activities. The conditional probability of having a heart attack given that you exercise daily may be smaller than the overall probability of having a heart attack. The conditional probability of having lung cancer given that you are a smoker is larger than the overall probability of having lung cancer. Note that changing the order of the conditional probability changes the meaning: the conditional probability of having lung cancer given that you are a smoker is a very different thing from the probability of being a smoker given that you have lung cancer. In an extreme case, suppose that a certain rare disease is caused only by eating a certain food, but even then, it is unlikely. Then the conditional probability of having that disease given that you eat the dangerous food is nonzero but low, but the conditional probability of having eaten that food given that you have the disease is 100%!

> **Review Video: Conditional Probability**
> Visit mometrix.com/academy and enter code: 397924

INDEPENDENCE

The conditional probability $P(A|B)$ is the probability that event A will occur given that event B occurs. If the two events are independent, we do not expect that whether or not event B occurs should have any effect on whether or not event A occurs. In other words, we expect $P(A|B) = P(A)$.

This can be proven using the usual equations for conditional probability and the joint probability of independent events. The conditional probability $P(A|B) = \frac{P(A \cap B)}{P(B)}$. If A and B are independent, then $P(A \cap B) = P(A)P(B)$. So $P(A|B) = \frac{P(A)P(B)}{P(B)} = P(A)$. By similar reasoning, if A and B are independent then $P(B|A) = P(B)$.

MULTIPLICATION RULE

The **multiplication rule** can be used to find the probability of two independent events occurring using the formula $P(A \cap B) = P(A) \times P(B)$, where $P(A \cap B)$ is the probability of two independent events occurring, $P(A)$ is the probability of the first event occurring, and $P(B)$ is the probability of the second event occurring.

The multiplication rule can also be used to find the probability of two dependent events occurring using the formula $P(A \cap B) = P(A) \times P(B|A)$, where $P(A \cap B)$ is the probability of two dependent events occurring and $P(B|A)$ is the probability of the second event occurring after the first event has already occurred.

Use a **combination of the multiplication** rule and the rule of complements to find the probability that at least one outcome of the element will occur. This is given by the general formula $P(\text{at least one event occurring}) = 1 - P(\text{no outcomes occurring})$. For example, to find the probability that at least one even number will show when a pair of dice is rolled, find the probability that two odd numbers will be rolled (no even numbers) and subtract from one. You can always use a tree diagram or make a chart to list the possible outcomes when the sample space is small, such as in the dice-rolling example, but in most cases it will be much faster to use the multiplication and complement formulas.

UNION AND INTERSECTION OF TWO SETS OF OUTCOMES

If A and B are each a set of elements or outcomes from an experiment, then the **union** (symbol ∪) of the two sets is the set of elements found in set A or set B. For example, if $A = \{2, 3, 4\}$ and $B = \{3, 4, 5\}$, $A \cup B = \{2, 3, 4, 5\}$. Note that the outcomes 3 and 4 appear only once in the union. For statistical events, the union is equivalent to "or"; $P(A \cup B)$ is the same thing as $P(A \text{ or } B)$. The **intersection** (symbol ∩) of two sets is the set of outcomes common to both sets. For the above sets A and B, $A \cap B = \{3, 4\}$. For statistical events, the intersection is equivalent to "and"; $P(A \cap B)$ is the same thing as $P(A \text{ and } B)$. It is important to note that union and intersection operations commute. That is:

$$A \cup B = B \cup A \text{ and } A \cap B = B \cap A$$

Permutations and Combinations in Probability

When trying to calculate the probability of an event using the $\frac{\text{desired outcomes}}{\text{total outcomes}}$ formula, you may frequently find that there are too many outcomes to individually count them. **Permutation** and **combination formulas** offer a shortcut to counting outcomes. A permutation is an arrangement of a specific number of a set of objects in a specific order. The number of **permutations** of r items given a set of n items can be calculated as $_nP_r = \frac{n!}{(n-r)!}$. Combinations are similar to permutations, except there are no restrictions regarding the order of the elements. While ABC is considered a different permutation than BCA, ABC and BCA are considered the same combination. The number of **combinations** of r items given a set of n items can be calculated as $_nC_r = \frac{n!}{r!(n-r)!}$ or $_nC_r = \frac{_nP_r}{r!}$.

Suppose you want to calculate how many different 5-card hands can be drawn from a deck of 52 cards. This is a combination since the order of the cards in a hand does not matter. There are 52 cards available, and 5 to be selected. Thus, the number of different hands is $_{52}C_5 = \frac{52!}{5! \times 47!} = 2{,}598{,}960$.

Tree Diagrams

For a simple sample space, possible outcomes may be determined by using a **tree diagram** or an organized chart. In either case, you can easily draw or list out the possible outcomes. For example, to determine all the possible ways three objects can be ordered, you can draw a tree diagram:

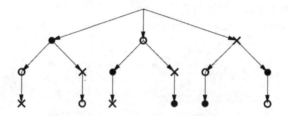

You can also make a chart to list all the possibilities:

First object	Second object	Third object
●	x	o
●	o	x
o	●	x
o	x	●
x	●	o
x	o	●

Either way, you can easily see there are six possible ways the three objects can be ordered.

If two events have no outcomes in common, they are said to be **mutually exclusive**. For example, in a standard deck of 52 playing cards, the event of all card suits is mutually exclusive to the event of all card values. If two events have no bearing on each other so that one event occurring has no influence on the probability of another event occurring, the two events are said to be independent. For example, rolling a standard six-sided die multiple times does not change that probability that a particular number will be rolled from one roll to the next. If the outcome of one event does affect the probability of the second event, the two events are said to be dependent. For example, if cards are drawn from a deck, the probability of drawing an ace after an ace has been drawn is different than the probability of drawing an ace if no ace (or no other card, for that matter) has been drawn.

In probability, the **odds in favor of an event** are the number of times the event will occur compared to the number of times the event will not occur. To calculate the odds in favor of an event, use the formula $\frac{P(A)}{1-P(A)}$, where $P(A)$ is the probability that the event will occur. Many times, odds in favor is given as a ratio in the form $\frac{a}{b}$ or $a:b$, where a is the probability of the event occurring and b is the complement of the event, the probability of the event not occurring. If the odds in favor are given as 2:5, that means that you can expect the event to occur two times for every 5 times that it does not occur. In other words, the probability that the event will occur is $\frac{2}{2+5} = \frac{2}{7}$.

In probability, the **odds against an event** are the number of times the event will not occur compared to the number of times the event will occur. To calculate the odds against an event, use the formula $\frac{1-P(A)}{P(A)}$, where $P(A)$ is the probability that the event will occur. Many times, odds against is given as a ratio in the form $\frac{b}{a}$ or $b:a$, where b is the probability the event will not occur (the complement of the event) and a is the probability the event will occur. If the odds against an event are given as 3:1, that means that you can expect the event to not occur 3 times for every one time it does occur. In other words, 3 out of every 4 trials will fail.

Two-Way Frequency Tables

If we have a two-way frequency table, it is generally a straightforward matter to read off the probabilities of any two events A and B, as well as the joint probability of both events occurring, $P(A \cap B)$. We can then find the conditional probability $P(A|B)$ by calculating $P(A|B) = \frac{P(A \cap B)}{P(B)}$. We could also check whether or not events are independent by verifying whether $P(A)P(B) = P(A \cap B)$.

For example, a certain store's recent T-shirt sales:

	Small	Medium	Large	Total
Blue	25	40	35	100
White	27	25	22	74
Black	8	23	15	46
Total	60	88	72	220

Suppose we want to find the conditional probability that a customer buys a black shirt (event A), given that the shirt he buys is size small (event B). From the table, the probability $P(B)$ that a customer buys a small shirt is $\frac{60}{220} = \frac{3}{11}$. The probability $P(A \cap B)$ that he buys a small, black shirt is $\frac{8}{220} = \frac{2}{55}$. The conditional probability $P(A|B)$ that he buys a black shirt, given that he buys a small shirt, is therefore $P(A|B) = \frac{2/55}{3/11} = \frac{2}{15}$.

Similarly, if we want to check whether the event a customer buys a blue shirt, A, is independent of the event that a customer buys a medium shirt, B. From the table, $P(A) = \frac{100}{220} = \frac{5}{11}$ and $P(B) = \frac{88}{220} = \frac{4}{10}$. Also, $P(A \cap B) = \frac{40}{220} = \frac{2}{11}$. Since $\left(\frac{5}{11}\right)\left(\frac{4}{10}\right) = \frac{20}{110} = \frac{2}{11}$, $P(A)P(B) = P(A \cap B)$ and these two events are indeed independent.

Expected Value

Expected value is a method of determining the expected outcome in a random situation. It is a sum of the weighted probabilities of the possible outcomes. Multiply the probability of an event occurring by the weight assigned to that probability (such as the amount of money won or lost). A practical application of the expected value is to determine whether a game of chance is really fair. If the sum of the weighted probabilities is equal to zero, the game is generally considered fair because the player has a fair chance to at least break even. If the expected value is less than zero, then players are expected to lose more than they win. For example, a lottery drawing might allow the player to choose any three-digit number, 000–999. The probability of choosing the winning number is 1:1000. If it costs \$1 to play, and a winning number receives \$500, the expected value is

$\left(-\$1 \times \frac{999}{1,000}\right) + \left(\$499 \times \frac{1}{1,000}\right) = -\$0.50$. You can expect to lose on average 50 cents for every dollar you spend.

EXPECTED VALUE AND SIMULATORS

A die roll simulator will show the results of n rolls of a die. The result of each die roll may be recorded. For example, suppose a die is rolled 100 times. All results may be recorded. The numbers of 1s, 2s, 3s, 4s, 5s, and 6s, may be counted. The experimental probability of rolling each number will equal the ratio of the frequency of the rolled number to the total number of rolls. As the number of rolls increases, or approaches infinity, the experimental probability will approach the theoretical probability of $\frac{1}{6}$. Thus, the expected value for the roll of a die is shown to be $\left(1 \times \frac{1}{6}\right) + \left(2 \times \frac{1}{6}\right) + \left(3 \times \frac{1}{6}\right) + \left(4 \times \frac{1}{6}\right) + \left(5 \times \frac{1}{6}\right) + \left(6 \times \frac{1}{6}\right)$, or 3.5.

Data Analysis

DISPERSION

A **measure of dispersion** is a single value that helps to "interpret" the measure of central tendency by providing more information about how the data values in the set are distributed about the measure of central tendency. The measure of dispersion helps to eliminate or reduce the disadvantages of using the mean, median, or mode as a single measure of central tendency, and give a more accurate picture of the dataset as a whole. To have a measure of dispersion, you must know or calculate the range, standard deviation, or variance of the data set.

RANGE

The **range** of a set of data is the difference between the greatest and lowest values of the data in the set. To calculate the range, you must first make sure the units for all data values are the same, and then identify the greatest and lowest values. If there are multiple data values that are equal for the highest or lowest, just use one of the values in the formula. Write the answer with the same units as the data values you used to do the calculations.

SAMPLE STANDARD DEVIATION

Standard deviation is a measure of dispersion that compares all the data values in the set to the mean of the set to give a more accurate picture. To find the **standard deviation of a sample**, use the formula

$$s = \sqrt{\frac{\sum_{i=1}^{n}(x_i - \bar{x})^2}{n-1}}$$

Note that s is the standard deviation of a sample, x_i represents the individual values in the data set, $\bar{x}$ is the mean of the data values in the set, and n is the number of data values in the set. The higher

the value of the standard deviation is, the greater the variance of the data values from the mean. The units associated with the standard deviation are the same as the units of the data values.

SAMPLE VARIANCE

The **variance of a sample** is the square of the sample standard deviation (denoted s^2). While the mean of a set of data gives the average of the set and gives information about where a specific data value lies in relation to the average, the variance of the sample gives information about the degree to which the data values are spread out and tells you how close an individual value is to the average compared to the other values. The units associated with variance are the same as the units of the data values squared.

PERCENTILE

Percentiles and quartiles are other methods of describing data within a set. **Percentiles** tell what percentage of the data in the set fall below a specific point. For example, achievement test scores are often given in percentiles. A score at the 80th percentile is one which is equal to or higher than 80 percent of the scores in the set. In other words, 80 percent of the scores were lower than that score.

Quartiles are percentile groups that make up quarter sections of the data set. The first quartile is the 25th percentile. The second quartile is the 50th percentile; this is also the median of the dataset. The third quartile is the 75th percentile.

SKEWNESS

Skewness is a way to describe the symmetry or asymmetry of the distribution of values in a dataset. If the distribution of values is symmetrical, there is no skew. In general the closer the mean of a data set is to the median of the data set, the less skew there is. Generally, if the mean is to the right of the median, the data set is *positively skewed*, or right-skewed, and if the mean is to the left of the median, the data set is *negatively skewed*, or left-skewed. However, this rule of thumb is not infallible. When the data values are graphed on a curve, a set with no skew will be a perfect bell curve.

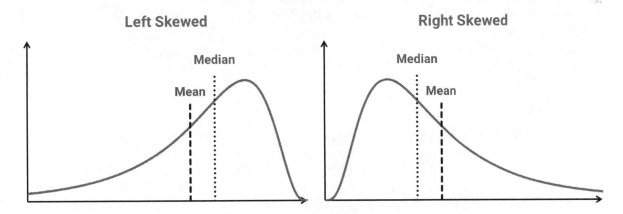

To estimate skew, use the formula:

$$\text{skew} = \frac{\sqrt{n(n-1)}}{n-2}\left(\frac{\frac{1}{n}\sum_{i=1}^{n}(x_i - \bar{x})^3}{\left(\frac{1}{n}\sum_{i=1}^{n}(x_i - \bar{x})^2\right)^{\frac{3}{2}}}\right)$$

Note that n is the datapoints in the set, x_i is the ith value in the set, and $\bar{x}$ is the mean of the set.

UNIMODAL VS. BIMODAL

If a distribution has a single peak, it would be considered **unimodal**. If it has two discernible peaks it would be considered **bimodal**. Bimodal distributions may be an indication that the set of data being considered is actually the combination of two sets of data with significant differences. A **uniform distribution** is a distribution in which there is *no distinct peak or variation* in the data. No values or ranges are particularly more common than any other values or ranges.

OUTLIER

An outlier is an extremely high or extremely low value in the data set. It may be the result of measurement error, in which case, the outlier is not a valid member of the data set. However, it may also be a valid member of the distribution. Unless a measurement error is identified, the experimenter cannot know for certain if an outlier is or is not a member of the distribution. There are arbitrary methods that can be employed to designate an extreme value as an outlier. One method designates an outlier (or possible outlier) to be any value less than $Q_1 - 1.5(IQR)$ or any value greater than $Q_3 + 1.5(IQR)$.

DATA ANALYSIS

SIMPLE REGRESSION

In statistics, **simple regression** is using an equation to represent a relation between independent and dependent variables. The independent variable is also referred to as the explanatory variable or the predictor and is generally represented by the variable x in the equation. The dependent variable, usually represented by the variable y, is also referred to as the response variable. The equation may be any type of function – linear, quadratic, exponential, etc. The best way to handle this task is to use the regression feature of your graphing calculator. This will easily give you the curve of best fit and provide you with the coefficients and other information you need to derive an equation.

LINE OF BEST FIT

In a scatter plot, the **line of best fit** is the line that best shows the trends of the data. The line of best fit is given by the equation $\hat{y} = ax + b$, where a and b are the regression coefficients. The regression coefficient a is also the slope of the line of best fit, and b is also the y-coordinate of the point at which the line of best fit crosses the y-axis. Not every point on the scatter plot will be on the line of best fit. The differences between the y-values of the points in the scatter plot and the corresponding y-values according to the equation of the line of best fit are the residuals. The line of best fit is also called the least-squares regression line because it is also the line that has the lowest sum of the squares of the residuals.

CORRELATION COEFFICIENT

The **correlation coefficient** is the numerical value that indicates how strong the relationship is between the two variables of a linear regression equation. A correlation coefficient of –1 is a perfect negative correlation. A correlation coefficient of +1 is a perfect positive correlation. Correlation coefficients close to –1 or +1 are very strong correlations. A correlation coefficient equal to zero indicates there is no correlation between the two variables. This test is a good indicator of whether or not the equation for the line of best fit is accurate. The formula for the correlation coefficient is

$$r = \frac{\sum_{i=1}^{n}(x_i - \bar{x})(y_i - \bar{y})}{\sqrt{\sum_{i=1}^{n}(x_i - \bar{x})^2}\sqrt{\sum_{i=1}^{n}(y_i - \bar{y})^2}}$$

where r is the correlation coefficient, n is the number of data values in the set, (x_i, y_i) is a point in the set, and $\bar{x}$ and $\bar{y}$ are the means.

Z-SCORE

A **z-score** is an indication of how many standard deviations a given value falls from the sample mean. To calculate a z-score, use the formula:

$$\frac{x - \bar{x}}{\sigma}$$

In this formula x is the data value, $\bar{x}$ is the mean of the sample data, and σ is the standard deviation of the population. If the z-score is positive, the data value lies above the mean. If the z-score is negative, the data value falls below the mean. These scores are useful in interpreting data such as standardized test scores, where every piece of data in the set has been counted, rather than just a small random sample. In cases where standard deviations are calculated from a random sample of the set, the z-scores will not be as accurate.

CENTRAL LIMIT THEOREM

According to the **central limit theorem**, regardless of what the original distribution of a sample is, the distribution of the means tends to get closer and closer to a normal distribution as the sample size gets larger and larger (this is necessary because the sample is becoming more all-encompassing of the elements of the population). As the sample size gets larger, the distribution of the sample mean will approach a normal distribution with a mean of the population mean and a variance of the population variance divided by the sample size.

Measures of Central Tendency

A **measure of central tendency** is a statistical value that gives a reasonable estimate for the center of a group of data. There are several different ways of describing the measure of central tendency. Each one has a unique way it is calculated, and each one gives a slightly different perspective on the data set. Whenever you give a measure of central tendency, always make sure the units are the same. If the data has different units, such as hours, minutes, and seconds, convert all the data to the same unit, and use the same unit in the measure of central tendency. If no units are given in the data, do not give units for the measure of central tendency.

MEAN

The **statistical mean** of a group of data is the same as the arithmetic average of that group. To find the mean of a set of data, first convert each value to the same units, if necessary. Then find the sum of all the values, and count the total number of data values, making sure you take into consideration each individual value. If a value appears more than once, count it more than once. Divide the sum of the values by the total number of values and apply the units, if any. Note that the mean does not have to be one of the data values in the set, and may not divide evenly.

$$\text{mean} = \frac{\text{sum of the data values}}{\text{quantity of data values}}$$

For instance, the mean of the data set {88, 72, 61, 90, 97, 68, 88, 79, 86, 93, 97, 71, 80, 84, 89} would be the sum of the fifteen numbers divided by 15:

$$\frac{88 + 72 + 61 + 90 + 97 + 68 + 88 + 79 + 86 + 93 + 97 + 71 + 80 + 84 + 89}{15} = \frac{1242}{15}$$
$$= 82.8$$

While the mean is relatively easy to calculate and averages are understood by most people, the mean can be very misleading if it is used as the sole measure of central tendency. If the data set has outliers (data values that are unusually high or unusually low compared to the rest of the data values), the mean can be very distorted, especially if the data set has a small number of values. If unusually high values are countered with unusually low values, the mean is not affected as much. For example, if five of twenty students in a class get a 100 on a test, but the other 15 students have an average of 60 on the same test, the class average would appear as 70. Whenever the mean is skewed by outliers, it is always a good idea to include the median as an alternate measure of central tendency.

A **weighted mean**, or weighted average, is a mean that uses "weighted" values. The formula is weighted mean $= \frac{w_1 x_1 + w_2 x_2 + w_3 x_3 \dots + w_n x_n}{w_1 + w_2 + w_3 + \dots + w_n}$. Weighted values, such as $w_1, w_2, w_3, \dots w_n$ are assigned to each member of the set $x_1, x_2, x_3, \dots x_n$. When calculating the weighted mean, make sure a weight value for each member of the set is used.

> **Review Video: All About Averages**
> Visit mometrix.com/academy and enter code: 176521

MEDIAN

The **statistical median** is the value in the middle of the set of data. To find the median, list all data values in order from smallest to largest or from largest to smallest. Any value that is repeated in the set must be listed the number of times it appears. If there are an odd number of data values, the median is the value in the middle of the list. If there is an even number of data values, the median is the arithmetic mean of the two middle values.

For example, the median of the data set {88, 72, 61, 90, 97, 68, 88, 79, 86, 93, 97, 71, 80, 84, 88} is 86 since the ordered set is {61, 68, 71, 72, 79, 80, 84, **86**, 88, 88, 88, 90, 93, 97, 97}.

The big disadvantage of using the median as a measure of central tendency is that is relies solely on a value's relative size as compared to the other values in the set. When the individual values in a set of data are evenly dispersed, the median can be an accurate tool. However, if there is a group of rather large values or a group of rather small values that are not offset by a different group of values, the information that can be inferred from the median may not be accurate because the distribution of values is skewed.

MODE

The **statistical mode** is the data value that occurs the greatest number of times in the data set. It is possible to have exactly one mode, more than one mode, or no mode. To find the mode of a set of data, arrange the data like you do to find the median (all values in order, listing all multiples of data values). Count the number of times each value appears in the data set. If all values appear an equal number of times, there is no mode. If one value appears more than any other value, that value is the mode. If two or more values appear the same number of times, but there are other values that appear fewer times and no values that appear more times, all of those values are the modes.

For example, the mode of the data set {**88**, 72, 61, 90, 97, 68, **88**, 79, 86, 93, 97, 71, 80, 84, **88**} is 88.

The main disadvantage of the mode is that the values of the other data in the set have no bearing on the mode. The mode may be the largest value, the smallest value, or a value anywhere in between in the set. The mode only tells which value or values, if any, occurred the greatest number of times. It does not give any suggestions about the remaining values in the set.

> **Review Video: Mean, Median, and Mode**
> Visit mometrix.com/academy and enter code: 286207

Displaying Information

FREQUENCY TABLES

Frequency tables show how frequently each unique value appears in a set. A **relative frequency table** is one that shows the proportions of each unique value compared to the entire set. Relative frequencies are given as percentages; however, the total percent for a relative frequency table will not necessarily equal 100 percent due to rounding. An example of a frequency table with relative frequencies is below.

Favorite Color	Frequency	Relative Frequency
Blue	4	13%
Red	7	22%
Green	3	9%
Purple	6	19%
Cyan	12	38%

> **Review Video: Data Interpretation of Graphs**
> Visit mometrix.com/academy and enter code: 200439

CIRCLE GRAPHS

Circle graphs, also known as *pie charts*, provide a visual depiction of the relationship of each type of data compared to the whole set of data. The circle graph is divided into sections by drawing radii to create central angles whose percentage of the circle is equal to the individual data's percentage of the whole set. Each 1% of data is equal to 3.6° in the circle graph. Therefore, data represented by a 90° section of the circle graph makes up 25% of the whole. When complete, a circle graph often looks like a pie cut into uneven wedges. The pie chart below shows the data from the frequency table referenced earlier where people were asked their favorite color.

Favorite Color

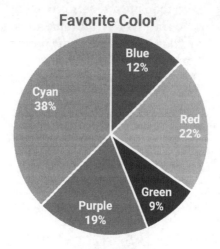

PICTOGRAPHS

A **pictograph** is a graph, generally in the horizontal orientation, that uses pictures or symbols to represent the data. Each pictograph must have a key that defines the picture or symbol and gives the quantity each picture or symbol represents. Pictures or symbols on a pictograph are not always shown as whole elements. In this case, the fraction of the picture or symbol shown represents the same fraction of the quantity a whole picture or symbol stands for. For example, a row with $3\frac{1}{2}$ ears of corn, where each ear of corn represents 100 stalks of corn in a field, would equal $3\frac{1}{2} \times 100 = 350$ stalks of corn in the field.

Name	Number of ears of corn eaten	Field	Number of stalks of corn
Michael	🌽🌽🌽🌽🌽	Field 1	🌽🌽🌽🌽🌽
Tara	🌽🌽	Field 2	🌽🌽🌽
John	🌽🌽🌽🌽	Field 3	🌽🌽🌽🌽
Sara	🌽	Field 4	🌽
Jacob	🌽🌽🌽	Field 5	🌽🌽🌽🌽

Each 🌽 represents 1 ear of corn eaten.   Each 🌽 represents 100 stalks of corn.

Review Video: Pictographs
Visit mometrix.com/academy and enter code: 147860

80

LINE GRAPHS

Line graphs have one or more lines of varying styles (solid or broken) to show the different values for a set of data. The individual data are represented as ordered pairs, much like on a Cartesian plane. In this case, the x- and y-axes are defined in terms of their units, such as dollars or time. The individual plotted points are joined by line segments to show whether the value of the data is increasing (line sloping upward), decreasing (line sloping downward), or staying the same (horizontal line). Multiple sets of data can be graphed on the same line graph to give an easy visual comparison. An example of this would be graphing achievement test scores for different groups of students over the same time period to see which group had the greatest increase or decrease in performance from year to year (as shown below).

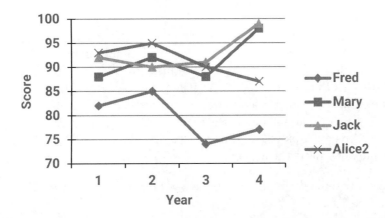

> **Review Video: How to Create a Line Graph**
> Visit mometrix.com/academy and enter code: 480147

LINE PLOTS

A **line plot**, also known as a *dot plot*, has plotted points that are not connected by line segments. In this graph, the horizontal axis lists the different possible values for the data, and the vertical axis lists the number of times the individual value occurs. A single dot is graphed for each value to show the number of times it occurs. This graph is more closely related to a bar graph than a line graph. Do not connect the dots in a line plot or it will misrepresent the data.

> **Review Video: Line Plot**
> Visit mometrix.com/academy and enter code: 754610

STEM AND LEAF PLOTS

A **stem and leaf plot** is useful for depicting groups of data that fall into a range of values. Each piece of data is separated into two parts: the first, or left, part is called the stem; the second, or right, part is called the leaf. Each stem is listed in a column from smallest to largest. Each leaf that has the common stem is listed in that stem's row from smallest to largest. For example, in a set of two-digit numbers, the digit in the tens place is the stem, and the digit in the ones place is the leaf. With a stem and leaf plot, you can easily see which subset of numbers (10s, 20s, 30s, etc.) is the largest. This information is also readily available by looking at a histogram, but a stem and leaf plot also allows you to look closer and see exactly which values fall in that range. Using a sample set of test scores (82, 88, 92, 93, 85, 90, 92, 95, 74, 88, 90, 91, 78, 87, 98, 99), we can assemble a stem and leaf plot like the one below.

Test Scores

7	4	8						
8	2	5	7	8	8			
9	0	0	1	2	2	3	5	8	9

BAR GRAPHS

A **bar graph** is one of the few graphs that can be drawn correctly in two different configurations – both horizontally and vertically. A bar graph is similar to a line plot in the way the data is organized on the graph. Both axes must have their categories defined for the graph to be useful. Rather than placing a single dot to mark the point of the data's value, a bar, or thick line, is drawn from zero to the exact value of the data, whether it is a number, percentage, or other numerical value. Longer bar lengths correspond to greater data values. To read a bar graph, read the labels for the axes to find the units being reported. Then, look where the bars end in relation to the scale given on the corresponding axis and determine the associated value.

The bar chart below represents the responses from our favorite-color survey.

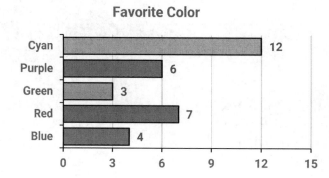

HISTOGRAMS

At first glance, a **histogram** looks like a vertical bar graph. The difference is that a bar graph has a separate bar for each piece of data and a histogram has one continuous bar for each *range* of data. For example, a histogram may have one bar for the range 0–9, one bar for 10–19, etc. While a bar graph has numerical values on one axis, a histogram has numerical values on both axes. Each range is of equal size, and they are ordered left to right from lowest to highest. The height of each column on a histogram represents the number of data values within that range. Like a stem and leaf plot, a histogram makes it easy to glance at the graph and quickly determine which range has the greatest quantity of values. A simple example of a histogram is below.

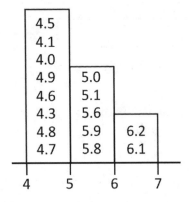

5-NUMBER SUMMARY

The **5-number summary** of a set of data gives a very informative picture of the set. The five numbers in the summary include the minimum value, maximum value, and the three quartiles. This information gives the reader the range and median of the set, as well as an indication of how the data is spread about the median.

BOX AND WHISKER PLOTS

A **box-and-whiskers plot** is a graphical representation of the 5-number summary. To draw a box-and-whiskers plot, plot the points of the 5-number summary on a number line. Draw a box whose ends are through the points for the first and third quartiles. Draw a vertical line in the box through the median to divide the box in half. Draw a line segment from the first quartile point to the minimum value, and from the third quartile point to the maximum value.

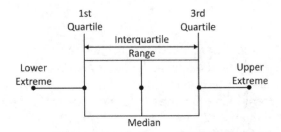

Review Video: Box and Whisker Plots
Visit mometrix.com/academy and enter code: 810817

EXAMPLE

Given the following data (32, 28, 29, 26, 35, 27, 30, 31, 27, 32), we first sort it into numerical order: 26, 27, 27, 28, 29, 30, 31, 32, 32, 35. We can then find the median. Since there are ten values, we take the average of the 5th and 6th values to get 29.5. We find the lower quartile by taking the median of the data smaller than the median. Since there are five values, we take the 3rd value, which is 27. We find the upper quartile by taking the median of the data larger than the overall median, which is 32. Finally, we note our minimum and maximum, which are simply the smallest and largest values in the set: 26 and 35, respectively. Now we can create our box plot:

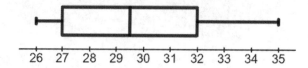

This plot is fairly "long" on the right whisker, showing one or more unusually high values (but not quite outliers). The other quartiles are similar in length, showing a fairly even distribution of data.

INTERQUARTILE RANGE

The **interquartile range, or IQR**, is the difference between the upper and lower quartiles. It measures how the data is dispersed: a high IQR means that the data is more spread out, while a low IQR means that the data is clustered more tightly around the median. To find the IQR, subtract the lower quartile value (Q_1) from the upper quartile value (Q_3).

EXAMPLE

To find the upper and lower quartiles, we first find the median and then take the median of all values above it and all values below it. In the following data set (16, 18, 13, 24, 16, 51, 32, 21, 27, 39), we first rearrange the values in numerical order: 13, 16, 16, 18, 21, 24, 27, 32, 39, 51. There are 10 values, so the median is the average of the 5th and 6th: $\frac{21+24}{2} = \frac{45}{2} = 22.5$. We do not actually need this value to find the upper and lower quartiles. We look at the set of numbers below the median: 13, 16, 16, 18, 21. There are five values, so the 3rd is the median (16), or the value of the lower quartile (Q_1). Then we look at the numbers above the median: 24, 27, 32, 39, 51. Again there are five values, so the 3rd is the median (32), or the value of the upper quartile (Q_3). We find the IQR by subtracting Q_1 from Q_3: $32 - 16 = 16$.

68-95-99.7 RULE

The **68–95–99.7 rule** describes how a normal distribution of data should appear when compared to the mean. This is also a description of a normal bell curve. According to this rule, 68 percent of the data values in a normally distributed set should fall within one standard deviation of the mean (34 percent above and 34 percent below the mean), 95 percent of the data values should fall within two standard deviations of the mean (47.5 percent above and 47.5 percent below the mean), and 99.7 percent of the data values should fall within three standard deviations of the mean, again, equally distributed on either side of the mean. This means that only 0.3 percent of all data values should fall more than three standard deviations from the mean. On the graph below, the normal curve is centered on the *y*-axis. The *x*-axis labels are how many standard deviations away from the center you are. Therefore, it is easy to see how the 68-95-99.7 rule can apply.

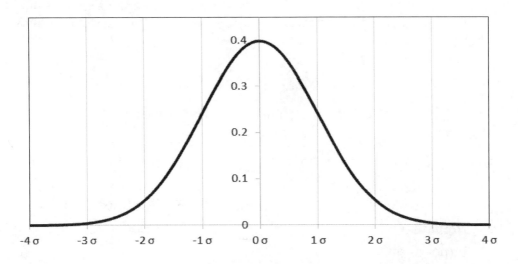

Scatter Plots

BIVARIATE DATA

Bivariate data is simply data from two different variables. (The prefix *bi-* means *two*.) In a *scatter plot*, each value in the set of data is plotted on a grid similar to a Cartesian plane, where each axis represents one of the two variables. By looking at the pattern formed by the points on the grid, you can often determine whether or not there is a relationship between the two variables, and what that relationship is, if it exists. The variables may be directly proportionate, inversely proportionate, or show no proportion at all. It may also be possible to determine if the data is linear, and if so, to find an equation to relate the two variables. The following scatter plot shows the relationship between preference for brand "A" and the age of the consumers surveyed.

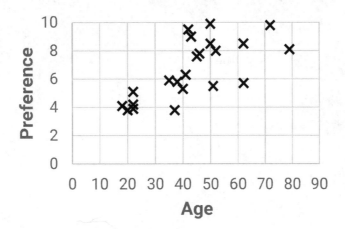

SCATTER PLOTS

Scatter plots are also useful in determining the type of function represented by the data and finding the simple regression. Linear scatter plots may be positive or negative. Nonlinear scatter plots are generally exponential or quadratic. Below are some common types of scatter plots:

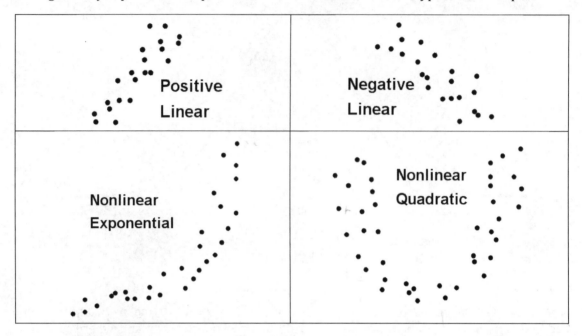

Keystone Practice Test #1

1. $f(x) = 5x + 10$. If $x = 10$, then what is the value of $f(x)$?
   a. 25
   b. 60
   c. 12
   d. 5

2. The table below lists values for x and $f(x)$.

x	f(x)
1	2
2	5
3	10
4	17
5	26

(handwritten annotations: +1 on each x row; +3 +2, +5 +2, +7 +2, +9 +2 on f(x) — "since this is equal, the function is quadratic")

Which of the following equations describes the relationship between x and $f(x)$?
   a. $f(x) = x + 1$ *not quadratic*
   b. $f(x) = x^2$ *doesn't fit data*
   c. $f(x) = (-x)^2$ *doesn't fit data*
   d. $f(x) = x^2 + 1$ *yes, it is quadratic and it works!*

3. What is $(x + 3)(2x - 5)$?
   a. $2x^2 + x + 15$
   b. $2x^2 + 11x - 15$
   c. $2x^2 + x - 15$
   d. $3x^2 + 11x + 15$

   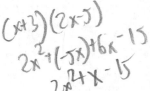
   (handwritten work: $(x+3)(2x-5)$, $2x^2 + (-5x) + 6x - 15$, $2x^2 + x - 15$)

4. Mrs. Rose has 16 students in her class. Her class has three times as many girls as boys. How many girls and boys are in Mrs. Rose's class?
   a. 12 girls, 4 boys
   b. 4 girls, 12 boys
   c. 3 girls, 1 boy
   d. 9 girls, 7 boys

   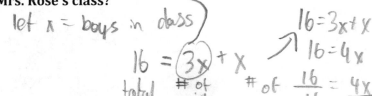
   (handwritten work: let x = boys in class; $16 = 3x + x$ total # of girls # of boys; $16 = 3x + x$, $16 = 4x$, $\frac{16}{4} = \frac{4x}{4}$, $4 = x$ boys; $3x =$, $3(4) = 12$ girls)

5. Which of the following is equivalent to $\sqrt{2^6}$?
   a. 8
   b. 32
   c. 2
   d. 4

   (handwritten work: If $\sqrt{x} = x^{1/2}$, $\sqrt{2^6} = (2^6)^{1/2}$; Since $(x^y)^z = x^{y \cdot z}$, $(2^6)^{1/2} = 2^{6 \cdot 1/2} = 2^3 = 8$)

87

6. Which of the following is equivalent to $\frac{24m^3n^2}{18m^2n^6}$?

a. $\frac{3m}{2n^4}$

b. $\frac{4mn^4}{3}$

c. $6m^5n^8$

d. $\frac{4m}{3n^4}$

$\frac{24}{18} = \frac{4}{3}$

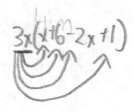

$\frac{24 \cdot m \cdot m \cdot m \cdot n \cdot n}{18 \cdot m \cdot m \cdot n \cdot n \cdot n \cdot n \cdot n \cdot n} \nearrow \frac{4m}{3n^4}$

7. Simplify: $3x(x + 6 - 2x + 1)$.

a. $-3x^2 + 21x$

b. $-3x^2 + 7$

c. $3x^2 - 6x^2 + 7$

d. $3x^2 - 21x$

$3x(x+6-2x+1)$

$3x^2 + 18x - 6x^2 + 3x$

$-3x^2 + 21x$

8. Which of these relations represents a function?

a.

x	3	7	1	5
y	−3	−5	−2	−4

+4 −6 +4

+2 +3 +2

✓

b.

+2 −2 −1

x	2	4	2	1
y	−1	4	1	0

+5 −3 −1

fails vertical line test

c.

x	−3	−3	−3	−3
y	1	2	3	4

fails vertical line test

d.

x	0	1	1	2
y	0	3	−3	6

fails vertical line test

9. If $f(x) = \frac{2}{3}x - 4$, what is the value of $f(-6)$?

a. −7

b. −4

c. −8

d. 0

$f(-6) = \frac{2}{3}(-6) - 4$

$f(-6) = -4 - 4$

$f(-6) = -8$

10. What is the 6th term of this arithmetic sequence?

$-6, -4, -2, 0, \ldots$

a. 4

b. 2

c. −8

d. 6

−6 −4 −2 0 2 4

+2 +2 +2 +2 +2

11. If $f(x) = x^2 - x - 3$, what is the value of $f(-1)$?

    a. −5
    b. −1
    c. −3
    d. −2

[handwritten: $f(-1) = (-1)^2 - (-1) - 3$ $f(-1) = 1 + 1 - 3$ $f(1) = 2 - 3$ $f(1) = -1$]

12. Which of the following formulas for the nth term corresponds to this arithmetic sequence?

    −8, −4, 0, 4, 8, …

    a. $a_n = 4n - 12$ *pass*
    b. $a_n = 4n - 4$ *fail*
    c. $a_n = -4n - 12$ *fail*
    d. $a_n = -4n - 4$ *fail*

13. Which of the following figures contains a graph of the function $y = 2x + 2$?

[handwritten: positive slop, y intercept]

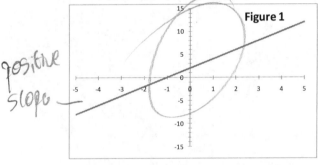

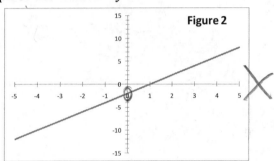

[handwritten: positive slope]

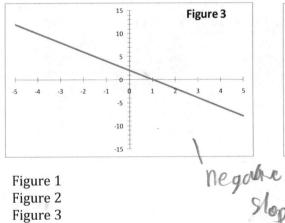

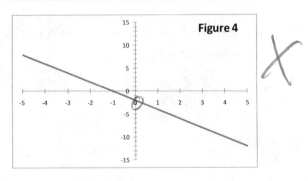

[handwritten: negative slop]

    a. Figure 1
    b. Figure 2
    c. Figure 3
    d. Figure 4

positive

y-intercept

14. Which of the following figures contains a graph of the function $y = x^2 + 10$**?**

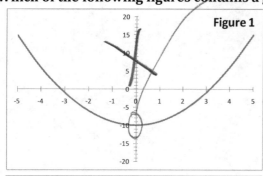

negative

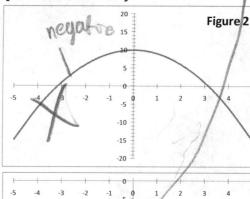

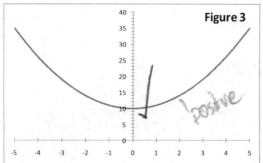

positive

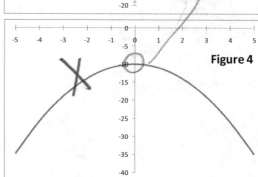

a. Figure 1
b. Figure 2
c. Figure 3
d. Figure 4

15. What is the correlation coefficient for the data in the table below?

The table shows the number of subs sold at Sam's Snack Shop the last several years.

Year	2010	2011	2012	2013	2014
Subs sold	222	263	302	345	394

+41   +39   +43   +59
+3   +4   +16

a. 0.899
b. 0.999
c. 0.875
d. 0.937

16. One study involving 9th grade students compared the number of hours spent watching television with the number of hours slept each night. Analysis of the data revealed a correlation coefficient of −0.920. Which of the following conclusions can be drawn from these data?

a. Watching more television causes students to sleep more hours each night.
b. Watching more television causes students to sleep fewer hours each night.
c. Watching more television is associated with more hours slept each night.
d. Watching more television is associated with fewer hours slept each night.

17. This table shows the price of a gallon of milk over several years.

Years since 2000	10	11	12	13	14
Price of milk	$2.17	$2.36	$2.57	$2.79	$2.99

Which of the following equations represents the best-fit line for these data?

a. $y = 0.207x + 0.092$
b. $y = 0.312x + 0.142$
c. $y = 0.427x + 0.339$
d. $y = 0.524x + 0.465$

Questions 18 and 19 pertain to the following coordinate pairs:

$$\{(-5, 18), (-2, 12), (0, 3), (2, -3), (5, -12)\}$$

18. What is the domain of the coordinate pairs?

a. $\{18, 12, 3, -3, -12\}$
b. $\{-5, -2, 0, 2, 5\}$
c. $\{0, 3\}$
d. $\{-5, 18, 5, -12\}$

19. What is the range of the coordinate pairs?

a. $\{18, 12, 3, -3, -12\}$
b. $\{-5, -2, 0, 2, 5\}$
c. $\{0, 3\}$
d. $\{-5, 18, 5, -12\}$

Questions 20 and 21 pertain to the following scenario:

Aisha runs a small business selling candy bars to her classmates in school. She buys each candy bar for $0.75, and she sells each candy bar for $1.50. Let y represent Aisha's profit. Let x represent the number of candy bars she sells per day.

20. Which equation best represents Aisha's daily profit from selling candy bars?

a. $y = 0.75x - 1.50x$
b. $y = 0.75x + 0.75x$
c. $y = 1.50x + 0.75x$
d. $y = 1.50x - 0.75x$

21. Which figure contains the graph that best represents Aisha's daily profit from selling candy bars?

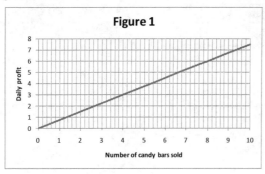

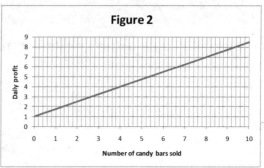

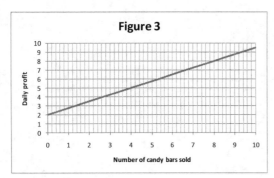

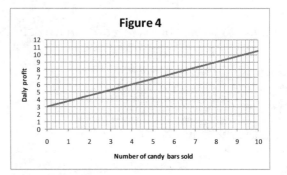

   a. Figure 1
   b. Figure 2
   c. Figure 3
   d. Figure 4

22. What are the factors of the following polynomial: $2x^2 + 7x - 15$?

 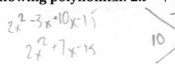

   a. $(2x + 5)(x - 3)$
   b. $(x + 5)(2x - 3)$
   c. $(2x - 5)(x + 3)$
   d. $(x - 5)(2x + 3)$

23. What is the solution to the following equation: $x^2 - 9 = 0$?

   a. $x = 3$
   b. $x = -3$
   c. Both A and B are solutions to the equation
   d. Neither A nor B is a solution to the equation

$x^2 = 9$

24. What is the simplest form of the following polynomial?

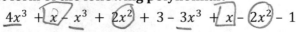

$$4x^3 + x - x^3 + 2x^2 + 3 - 3x^3 + x - 2x^2 - 1$$

   a. $2x + 2$
   b. $x + 1$
   c. $x^3 + 1$
   d. $2(x + 1)$

$2x + 2$

25. Which of the following equations is an example of the distributive property?
    a. $(5)(3) = (3)(5)$
    b. $5 + 3 = 3 + 5$
    c. $(5)(1 + 2) = (5)(1) + (5)(2)$
    d. $15 = 15$

26. Which of the following binomials can be rewritten as a difference of squares with rational coefficients?
    a. $16x^2 + 4$
    b. $9x^2 - 12x + 4$
    c. $4x^2 - y^2$
    d. $8x^3 + 16$

$(4x-y)^2$ $16x2$

27. Which of the following is the value of x when $3 < -\frac{1}{2}x + 1$?
    a. $x < 4$
    b. $x > 4$
    c. $x < -4$
    d. $x > -4$

$2 \le -\frac{1}{2}x$

$-4 \ge x$

28. John noticed that the number of points he scores during a basketball game is directly related to the number of hours he spends practicing each week. The table below lists John's weekly scores as a function of hours practiced. Let h represent the number of hours practiced and let p represent the number of points scored. Which equation represents the number of points John scored as a function of the number of hours he practiced?

Number of hours practiced	Number of points scored during basketball game
2	11
4	21
6	31
8	41
10	51

    a. $p(h) = 5h + 1$
    b. $p(h) = 5h - 1$
    c. $p(h) = p + 10$
    d. $p(h) = p - 10$

29. Which of the following is parallel to the line $2x + 3y - 6 = 0$ and goes through the point $(6, 0)$?
    a. $y = -\frac{2}{3}x + 4$
    b. $y = -\frac{3}{2}x - 2$
    c. $y = \frac{2}{3}x$
    d. $y = \frac{3}{2}x - 7$

$\frac{-2 \cdot 6^2}{3 \cdot 1} = -4 + 4$

$\frac{-3 \cdot 6^3}{2 \cdot 1} = -9$

$\frac{3 \cdot 6^3}{2 \cdot 1} = -9$

93

30. What is the equation of the line that is perpendicular to $y = 3x - 8$ and passes through the point (–3,2)?

    a. $y = 3x + 11$

    b. $y = \frac{1}{3}x + 3$

    c. $y = -\frac{1}{3}x + 3$

    d. $y = -\frac{1}{3}x + 1$

Questions 31 and 32 pertain to the following graph:

The graph describes the change in distance over time for a particular car.

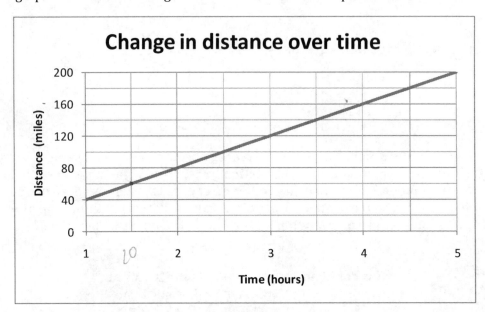

31. What is the slope of the line shown in the graph?

    a. 20

    b. 40

    c. 60

    d. 80

32. What are the units of the slope of the line?

    a. time per distance

    b. distance per time

    c. hours per miles

    d. miles per hour

Questions 33 and 34 pertain to the following information:

    Let Equation A: $5y - 100x = 25$
    Let Equation B: $5y - 200x = 75$

$5y = 200x + 75$

$y = 40x + 15$

$5y = 100x + 25$

$y = 20x + 5$

33. How does the slope of Equation B compare to the slope of Equation A?

a. The slope of Equation B is half the slope of Equation A.
b. The slope of Equation B is twice the slope of Equation A.
c. The slope of Equation B is 200 times the slope of Equation A.
d. The slope of Equation B is the same as the slope of the Equation A.

34. How does the y-intercept of Equation B compare to the y-intercept of Equation A?

a. The y-intercept of Equation B is twice the y-intercept of Equation A.
b. The y-intercept of Equation B is three times the y-intercept of Equation A.
c. The y-intercept of Equation B is 75 times the y-intercept of Equation A.
d. The y-intercept of Equation B is the same as the y-intercept of Equation A.

35. Line M contains the following two points: (1, 10) and (6, 20). What is the slope of line M?

a. 5
b. 2
c. 0.5
d. 10

$\frac{10}{5} = 2$

36. Line Q has a slope of 10 and intercepts the y-axis at point (0, –15). What is the equation of line Q?

a. $y = -15$
b. $y = -15x + 10$
c. $y = 15x - 10$
d. $y = 10x - 15$

37. The equation for line 1 is $y_1 = 2x_1 + 6$ and the equation for line 2 is $y_2 = -x_2 - 3$. At what point does line 1 intersect line 2?

a. $(-3, 6)$
b. $(6, -3)$
c. $(-3, 0)$
d. $(0, -3)$

$y=2x+6$ $\quad$ $y=-x-3$

$2y=-2x-6$

$3y=0$ $\quad$ $3y=$

38. Table A below contains the *x*- and *y*-coordinates for several points on line *P*. Table B contains the *x*- and *y*-coordinates for several points on line *Q*. At what point does line *P* intersect line *Q*?

Table A: Coordinates for line *P*	
x	*y*
−5	−8
−4	−4
−3	0
−2	4
−1	8
0	12
1	16

Table B: Coordinates for line *Q*	
x	*y*
−5	4
−4	2
−3	0
−2	−2
−1	−4
0	−6
1	−8

a. (−3, 0)
b. (−5, −8)
c. (0, −6)
d. (1, −8)

39. If $f(x) = 3x - 8$, how would the function be affected by replacing $f(x)$ with $f(x + 2)$?
   a. The graph would move two units to the right.
   b. The graph would move two units to the left. ⟵
   c. The graph would move two units to the right and two units up.
   d. The graph would move two units to the left and two units up.

Questions 40 and 41 pertain to the following information:

Elli wants to plant a flower garden that contains only roses and tulips. However, she has a limited amount of space for the garden, and she can only afford to buy a specific number of each plant. Elli has enough space to plant a total of 20 flowers, and she has a total of $100 to purchase the flowers. Roses cost $14 per plant and tulips cost $4 per plant. Let *R* represent the number of roses and let *T* represent the number of tulips Elli will plant in her garden.

40. How many tulips will Elli plant in her flower garden?
   a. 4
   b. 20
   c. 18
   d. 2

$R+T=20 \qquad 14R+4T=100$

$4r+4t=80$

$10R=20 \qquad R=2$

41. Suppose the local greenhouse has a sale, allowing Elli to purchase roses for $9 per plant. Now how many roses and tulips will Elli plant in her garden?
   a. 4 roses and 16 tulips
   b. 16 roses and 4 tulips
   c. 9 roses and 11 tulips
   d. 20 roses and 0 tulips

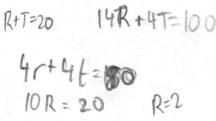

$R+T=20.$

$14 \qquad 9R+4T=100$

$6 \qquad 5R=20$

4

Questions 42 and 43 pertain to the following information:

Joshua has to earn more than 92 points on the state test in order to qualify for an academic scholarship. Each question is worth 4 points, and the test has a total of 30 questions. Let *x* represent the number of test questions.

42. Which of the following inequalities can be solved to determine the number of questions Joshua must answer correctly?

a. $4x < 30$
b. $4x < 92$
c. $4x > 30$
d. $4x > 92$

43. How many questions must Joshua answer correctly?

a. $x < 30$
b. $x < 23$
c. $23 < x < 30$
d. $23 < x \leq 30$

Questions 44 and 45 pertain to the following information:

$$y_1 = x^2 \qquad y_2 = -x^2 \qquad y_3 = x^2 + 10$$

44. Which of the following numbers is included in the range of y_1?

a. 0
b. −1
c. −2
d. −3

45. How does function y_2 compare to the original function y_1?

a. y_2 has a different domain than y_1
b. y_2 has a different range than y_1
c. y_2 is shifted vertically by −1 unit when compared to y_1
d. y_2 is shifted horizontally by −1 unit when compared to y_1

46. A ball is dropped from a window 35 feet off the ground. Two seconds after dropping, the ball is 5 feet off the ground. If the height (*h*) in feet of the ball is modeled as a quadratic function of time (*t*) in seconds which of these functions represents this situation?

a. $h = -15t^2 + 30$
b. $h = -30t^2 + 35$
c. $h = -30t^2 + 30$
d. $h = -15t^2 + 35$

 $4 \quad -30$

47. What is the equation of the parabola with vertex (0, 0) that passes through (−2, 8)?

a. $y = (2x)^2$
b. $y = 2(x + 2)^2$
c. $y = 2x^2$
d. $y = (x + 2)^2$

48. What is the equation of the parabola with vertex (−3, −6) that passes through (0, 3)?

    a. $y = (x - 3)^2 - 6$
    b. $y = (x - 6)^2 - 3$
    c. $y = (x + 3)^2 - 6$
    d. $y = (x + 3)^2 + 6$

49. What is the equation of a parabola that is symmetrical about the *y*-axis and goes through the points (0, −3) and (2, 5)?

    a. $y = 2x^2 - 3$
    b. $y = 2x^2$
    c. $y = 3x^2 - 3$
    d. $y = x^2 + 3$

50. At what value for *x* does the equation $x^2 + 10x = -25$ intercept the *x*-axis? Write your answer in the answer grid.

− / +	0	0
	1	1
	2	2
	3	3
	4	4
	5	5
	6	6
	7	7
	8	8
	9	9

98

51. Consider the following equations:

$$x^2 = 4 \qquad x^3 = -8 \qquad x^4 = 16 \qquad x^5 = -32$$

What is x? Write your answer in the answer grid.

(−)	0	0
+	1	1
/	(2)	2
	3	3
	4	4
	5	5
	6	6
	7	7
	8	8
	9	9

52. Let y be inversely proportional to x such that $y = -\frac{1}{6}x$. If $y = 5$, what is x? Write your answer in the answer grid.

(−)	0	(0)
+	1	1
	2	2
	(3)	3
	4	4
	5	5
	6	6
	7	7
	8	8
	9	9

$$5 =$$

$$5 \cdot \frac{-6}{1} = -30$$

53. Solve the following equation for x:

$$2^x = 65,536$$

Write your answer in the answer grid.

–	0	0
+	1	1
	2	2
	3	3
	4	4
	5	5
	6	6
	7	7
	8	8
	9	9

54. What is the sum of all values of x that satisfy the following equation?

$$3x^2 - 3x - 34 = 2$$

    a. −3
    b. 0
    c. 1
    d. 4

$3x^2 - 3x - 36$

$3(x^2 - x - 12)$ $(x-3)(x+4)$

55. What are the domain and range of $y = \left(\frac{1}{2}\right)^x$?

    a. The domain is $-2 \le x$, and the range is $y < 2$.
    b. The domain is $0 \le x < +\infty$, and the range is $-2 < y < +\infty$.
    c. The domain is $-\infty < x < +\infty$, and the range is $-\infty < y < +\infty$.
    d. The domain is $-\infty < x < +\infty$, and the range is $0 < y < +\infty$.

−decay

56. Which of the following statements is true regarding the equation $y = 3(2)^x$?

    a. This is a quadratic function.
    b. This is a linear function.
    c. This is an exponential growth function.
    d. This is an exponential decay function.

57. Which of the following statements must be true about an exponential growth function in the form of $y = ab^x$?

    a. $b > 1$
    b. $b < 1$
    c. $a > 1$
    d. $a < 1$

58. What is the *y*-intercept of this graph of $y = 2(3^x)$?

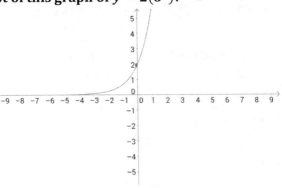

   a. $(0, 0)$
   b. $(0, 2)$
   c. $(2, 0)$
   d. $(2, 2)$

59. What is the *y*-intercept of the graph of $y = 6\left(\frac{1}{2}\right)^x$?

   a. $(0, -6)$
   b. $(0, 3)$
   c. $(6, 0)$
   d. $(0, 6)$

60. The population of a growing city in the 1940s is given in the table below. Use a graphing calculator to write an exponential function to model this growth. Which of the following is the best prediction of the population of this town in 1950?

Year	Population
1940	22,245
1941	23,357
1942	24,524
1943	25,750
1944	27,038

   a. 34,710
   b. 35,960
   c. 36,230
   d. 37,490

Answer Key and Explanations for Test #1

1. B: The equation describes a functional relationship between x and $f(x)$. To solve the equation, substitute 10 as the value of x, such that $f(10) = 5(10) + 10 = 50 + 10 = 60$. Therefore, choice B is correct.

2. D: For each value of x, $f(x) = x^2 + 1$,

$$f(1) = (1)^2 + 1 = (1)(1) + 1 = 1 + 1 = 2$$
$$f(2) = (2)^2 + 1 = (2)(2) + 1 = 4 + 1 = 5$$
$$f(3) = (3)^2 + 1 = (3)(3) + 1 = 9 + 1 = 10$$
$$f(4) = (4)^2 + 1 = (4)(4) + 1 = 16 + 1 = 17$$
$$f(5) = (5)^2 + 1 = (5)(5) + 1 = 25 + 1 = 26$$

Therefore, choice D is correct.

3. C: Applying the distributive property results in $x(2x) + x(-5) + 3(2x) + 3(-5)$. Simplifying the expression yields $2x^2 - 5x + 6x - 15$. Collecting like terms yields $2x^2 + x - 15$. Therefore, choice C is correct.

4. A: Let x represent the number of boys in Mrs. Rose's class. Since Mrs. Rose has three times as many girls in her class as boys, $3x$ represents the number of girls in Mrs. Rose's class. The total number of students in the class is 16. Written as an equation and solved for x we get:

$$x + 3x = 16$$
$$4x = 16$$
$$x = 4$$

Hence $x = 4$ and $3x = 12$. Therefore, 4 is the number of boys and 12 is the number of girls. Also, $4 + 12 = 16$, the total number of students in the class. Therefore, choice A is correct.

5. A: The radical $\sqrt{2^6}$ can be rewritten as $2^{\frac{6}{2}}$ which is equal to 2^3 or 8. Therefore, choice A is correct.

6. D: When dividing expressions with exponents, the exponents of like bases are subtracted. The coefficients are divided. In this case, the fraction formed by the coefficients in the numerator and the denominator can be reduced. For the problem $\frac{24m^3n^2}{18m^2n^6}$, the quotient is $\frac{4m}{3n^4}$. Therefore, choice D is correct.

7. A: First simplify the terms inside the parentheses: $x + 6 - 2x + 1 = -x + 7$. Then use the distributive property to simplify, multiplying $3x$ by each term inside the parentheses: $3x(-x + 7) = -3x^2 + 21x$. Therefore, choice A is correct.

8. A: A relation is a function when each input has only one output. In this case, the relation is a function when each x-value has only one y-value. In choice B, $x = 2$ has two y-values. In choice C, $x = -3$ has four y-values. In choice D, $x = 1$ has two y-values. Therefore, choice A is correct.

9. C: To solve, substitute $x = -6$ into $f(x) = \frac{2}{3}x - 4$. Then $f(-6) = \frac{2}{3}(-6) - 4 = 2(-2) - 4 = -4 - 4 = -8$. Therefore, choice C is correct.

102

10. A: An arithmetic sequence increases or decreases at a constant rate. The intervals between the terms is a common difference. The common difference for this sequence is +2. The next three terms in this sequence are 2, 4, and 6. The 6th term is 4. Therefore, choice A is correct.

11. B: To solve, substitute $x = -1$ into $f(x) = x^2 - x - 3$. Then $f(-1) = (-1)^2 - (-1) - 3 = 1 + 1 - 3 = 2 - 3 = -1$. Therefore, choice B is correct.

12. A: The nth term of an arithmetic sequence is found by $a_n = a_1 + (n-1)d$ where d represents the common difference. The common difference for this sequence is +4. Then $a_n = -8 + (n-1)(4) = -8 + 4n - 4 = 4n - 12$. Therefore, choice A is correct.

13. A: The equation is written in the form of the point slope formula: $y = mx + b$ where m is the slope of the line and b is the y-axis intercept. For the given equation $y = 2x + 2$, the slope of the line is positive 2 and the line intercepts the y-axis at positive 2. The graph in Figure 1 fits these criteria. The graph in Figure 2 intercepts the y-axis at negative 2. The graphs in Figure 3 and Figure 4 have slopes of negative 2. Therefore, choice A is correct.

14. C: The equation is written in the form $y = Ax^2 + B$ where A tells the concavity of the graph and B is the y-intercept. In this case, A equals positive 1. So the graph is concave up. B equals positive 10. So the graph intercepts the y-axis at positive 10. The graph in Figure 3 fits these criteria. The graph in Figure 1 intercepts the y-axis at negative 10. The graphs in Figure 2 and Figure 4 are concave down. Therefore, choice C is correct.

15. B: Use a graphing calculator. Press STAT and select EDIT to enter the *year* data into List 1. Enter the *Subs sold* data into List 2. To perform the regression, press STAT and select CALC. Scroll down to LinReg(ax+b). The r value is the correlation coefficient. Therefore, choice B is correct. (Different graphing calculators might involve slightly different procedures; consult the instructions to your calculator.)

16. D: Since the correlation coefficient is close to −1, there is a strong negative correlation between the variables. Watching more television is associated with fewer hours slept each night. However, correlation does not imply causation. Therefore, choice D is correct.

17. A: Use a graphing calculator. Press STAT and select EDIT to enter the *Years since 2000* data into List 1. Enter the *Price of milk* data into List 2. To perform the regression, press STAT and select CALC. Scroll down to LinReg(ax+b). (Different graphing calculators might involve slightly different procedures; consult the instructions to your calculator.) With an equation in the form of $y = ax + b$, $a = 0.207$ and $b = 0.092$. Then the equation is $y = 0.207x + 0.092$. Therefore, choice A is correct.

18. B: The list of coordinate pairs represents the x- and y-values of five points. The domain is all the x-values. Answer B contains all the x-values of the coordinate pairs. Therefore, choice B is correct.

19. A: The list of coordinate pairs represents the x- and y-values of five points. The range is all the y-values. Answer A contains all the y-values of the coordinate pairs. Therefore, choice A is correct.

20. D: To calculate Aisha's daily profit, first determine the amount of money Aisha earns from selling candy. Since x represents the number of candy bars she sells per day, and she sells each bar for $1.50, then her daily earnings equal $1.50x$. Next, determine how much money Aisha spends buying the candy. Since each bar costs $0.75, she spends a total of $0.75x$ buying the candy. Finally, subtract the amount of money she spends buying the candy from the amount of money she earns selling the candy. Since y represents her daily profits, $y = 1.50x - 0.75x$. Therefore, choice D is correct.

21. A: The graph that represents Aisha's daily profit can be determined from the equation $y = 1.50x - 0.75x$. This equation can also be written as $y = (1.50 - 0.75)x$ or $y = 0.75x$. In its simplest form, the equation that describes Aisha's profits has a y-intercept of 0 and a slope of 0.75. The y-intercept tells the profits Aisha will earn if she sells no candy bars. Based on the equation, if Aisha sells no candy bars, then she earns no profit. The graph in Figure 1 fits these criteria. Therefore, choice A is correct.

22. B: To factor the polynomial, find factors of the first and third terms whose product can be added to get the middle term. The fastest way to find the correct answer is to multiply the answer choices and select the choice that yields the original equation. In this case,

$$(x + 5)(2x - 3) = (x)(2x) + (x)(-3) + (5)(2x) + (5)(-3)$$

$$= 2x^2 - 3x + 10x - 15$$

$$= 2x^2 + 7x - 15$$

Therefore, choice B is correct.

23. C: The solution to the equation follows:

$$x^2 - 9 = 0$$
$$x^2 = 9$$
$$x = \sqrt{9}$$

$$x = +3 \; and \; x = -3$$

Therefore, choice C is correct.

24. D: To simplify the polynomial, group and combine all terms of the same order.

$$4x^3 + x - x^3 + 2x^2 + 3 - 3x^3 + x - 2x^2 - 1$$

$$= (4x^3 - x^3 - 3x^3) + (2x^2 - 2x^2) + (x + x) + (3 - 1)$$

$$= 0 + 0 + 2x + 2$$

$$= 2(x + 1)$$

Therefore, choice D is correct.

25. C: The distributive property says that terms inside a set of parentheses can be multiplied by a factor outside the parentheses. In other words, $a(b + c) = ab + ac$. Answer C fits this definition.

26. C: The difference of two squares is written in the form $a^2 - b^2$, which can be factored as $(a - b)(a + b)$. Of the answer choices, $4x^2 - y^2$ can be factored into $(2x - y)(2x + y)$. Therefore, choice C is correct.

27. C: To solve, we first subtract 1 from each side: $3 < -\frac{1}{2}x + 1 \rightarrow 2 < -\frac{1}{2}x$. Then multiply each side by –2 (note that changing the sign involves flipping the inequality): $2 < -\frac{1}{2}x \rightarrow -4 > x$. Then we can simply rewrite this as $x < -4$. To test, we can choose any number less than –4, such as –6, and substitute for x in the original equation: $3 < -\frac{1}{2}(-6) + 1 \rightarrow 3 < 3 + 1 \rightarrow 3 < 4$. This is true, so the equation seems to be true. We can further test by choosing a number outside the range, such as 0: $3 < -\frac{1}{2}(0) + 1$. Since 3 is not less than 1, this is not true, further verifying the answer. Therefore, choice C is correct.

28. A: In each case, the number of points scored p equals $5(h) + 1$ where h is the number of hours practiced. For example, $11 = (5)(2) + 1$ and $21 = (5)(4) + 1$. For answers C and D, the points scored are not written as functions of the hours practiced. Therefore, choice A is correct.

29. A: Two parallel lines have the same slope, so we first rearrange the original equation into point-slope form to find the slope. First, subtract $2x - 6$ from each side: $3y = -2x + 6$. Then divide each side by 3: $y = -\frac{2}{3}x + 2$. The slope is $-\frac{2}{3}$. Now we find the y-intercept by using the point $(6, 0)$ in the slope-intercept equation $y = mx + b$: $0 = -\frac{2}{3}(6) + b$. Solving this yields $b = 4$, so the equation is $y = -\frac{2}{3}x + 4$. Therefore, choice A is correct.

30. D: When a line is perpendicular to another, its slope is the negative reciprocal of the other. The slope of the original equation is 3, so the slope of the perpendicular line is $-\frac{1}{3}$. To find the y-intercept, write the equation in slope-intercept form and substitute the given point: $2 = -\frac{1}{3}(-3) + b$, where b is the y-intercept. We solve for b: $2 = 1 + b$, so $b = 1$. The final equation is $y = -\frac{1}{3}x + 1$. Therefore, choice D is correct.

31. B: The slope of a line describes the change in the dependent variable divided by the change in the independent variable, i.e. the change in y over the change in x. To calculate the slope, consider any two points on the line. Let the first point be $(1, 40)$ and let the second point be $(2, 80)$:

$$\frac{y_2 - y_1}{x_2 - x_1} = \frac{80 - 40}{2 - 1} = \frac{40}{1} = 40$$

Therefore, choice B is correct.

32. D: The slope of the line is the change in y divided by the change in x. Therefore, the units of the slope are the units of y over the units for x. The unit for y is the unit for distance or miles. The unit for x is the unit for time or hours. Hence the units of the slope are miles over hours or miles per hour. Therefore, choice D is correct.

33. B: Write Equation B in slope-intercept form, which is $y = mx + b$:

$$5y - 200x = 75$$
$$5y = 200x + 75$$
$$y = 40x + 15$$

Now write Equation A in slope-intercept form:

$$5y - 100x = 25$$
$$5y = 100x + 25$$
$$y = 20x + 5$$

Since the slope Equation B is 40 and the slope of Equation A is 20, the slope of Equation B is twice the slope of Equation A. Therefore, choice B is correct.

34. B: Based on the slope-intercept form, which is $y = mx + b$, the y-intercept of Equation B is 15 and the y-intercept of Equation A is 5, so the y-intercept of Equation B is three time the y-intercept of Equation A. Therefore, choice B is correct.

35. B: The slope of a line is the change in y divided by the change in x. Calculate the slope as follows:

$$m = \frac{y_2 - y_1}{x_2 - x_1} = \frac{20 - 10}{6 - 1} = \frac{10}{5} = 2$$

Therefore, choice B is correct.

36. D: Write the equation in slope-intercept form: $y = mx + b$ where m is the slope of the line and b is the y-intercept. In this case, the slope $m = 10$ and the y-intercept $b = -15$. Hence $y = 10x - 15$. Therefore, choice D is correct.

37. C: At the intersection point of line 1 and line 2, $y_1 = y_2 = y$ and $x_1 = x_2 = x$. To find the x-coordinate, let $y_1 = y_2$.

$$\begin{aligned} 2x + 6 &= -x - 3 \\ 2x + x &= -6 - 3 \\ 3x &= -9 \\ x &= -3 \end{aligned}$$

Now find the y-coordinate by substituting $x = -3$ into either the equation for line 1 or the equation for line 2.

$$\begin{aligned} y &= 2x + 6 \\ y &= (2)(-3) + 6 \\ y &= -6 + 6 \\ y &= 0 \end{aligned}$$

Therefore, the point of intersection is $(-3, 0)$ and choice C is correct.

38. A: The intersection point of line P and line Q will be common to both lines (see the explanation for question 34). Point $(-3, 0)$ is the only point that is common to both lines. Therefore, choice A is correct.

39. B: The parent function is a line that intersects the y-axis at $(0, 8)$. Substituting $x+2$ for x shifts this parabola two units to the left, but does not affect the y-intercept. Therefore, choice B is correct.

40. C: The total number of plants is 20, so we can write this as $R + T = 20$. Since roses cost \$14 each and tulips cost \$4 each, for a total cost of \$100, we can write this as $14R + 4T = 100$. We can solve this system of equations by substitution. First we need to rewrite the first equation:

$$R + T = 20$$

$$-R \qquad = -R$$

$$T = 20 - R$$

Now we can combine the two equations, substituting the equation above for T:

$$14R + 4(20 - R) = 100$$

$$14R + 80 - 4R = 100$$

$$10R = 20$$

$$R = 2$$

Now we can solve for T by referring to our original first equation:

$$R + T = 20$$

$$2 + T = 20$$

$$T = 18$$

Thus, Elli will plant 18 tulips in her garden. Therefore, choice C is correct.

41. A: The new price for roses requires defining a new system of equations. Elli will still plant a total of 20 flowers. Hence

$$R + T = 20$$
$$T = 20 - R$$

However, based on the new price for roses,

$$9R + 4T = 100$$
$$9R + 4(20 - R) = 100$$
$$9R + 80 - 4R = 100$$
$$5R = 20$$
$$R = 4$$

At the new price for roses, Elli will plant 4 roses in her garden. Since $R + T = 20$, Elli will plant 16 tulips in her garden. Therefore, choice A is correct.

42. D: In order to determine the number of questions Joshua must answer correctly, consider the number of points he must earn. Joshua will receive 4 points for each question he answers correctly, and x represents the number of questions. Therefore, Joshua will receive a total of $4x$ points for all the questions he answers correctly. Joshua must earn more than 92 points. Therefore, to determine the number of questions he must answer correctly, solve the inequality $4x > 92$. Therefore, choice D is correct.

43. D: See the explanation for the previous question. To determine the number of questions Joshua must correctly answer, solve the following inequality:

$$4x > 92$$

$$x > \frac{92}{4}$$

$$x > 23$$

Therefore, Joshua must correctly answer more than 23 questions to qualify for the scholarship. Because the test has a total of 30 questions, Joshua could answer as many as 30 questions correctly. Hence, the best inequality to describe the number of questions Joshua must correctly answer is $23 < x \leq 30$. Therefore, choice D is correct.

44. A: The range is all the y-values. Refer to a graph of y_1 shown below.

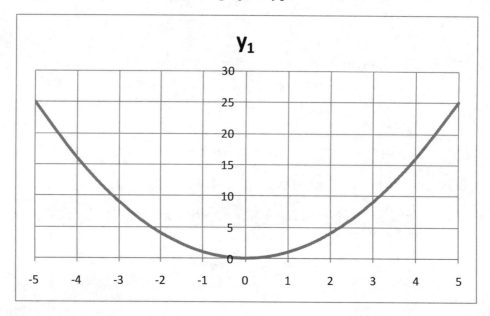

The minimum value for y is 0. Another way to solve this problem is to substitute the potential y-values in the equation for y_1. For example,

$$y_1 = x^2$$
$$-1 = x^2$$
$$\sqrt{-1} = x$$

This statement has no real solution since it requires taking the square root of a negative number. Similar solutions are obtained for $y = -2$ or $y = -3$. Therefore, choice A is correct.

45. B: The original function y_1 is concave up (see the graph of y_1 shown in the explanation for problem 46). Changing the coefficient of x^2 from +1 to –1 causes the function to be concave down. See the graph of y_2 shown below.

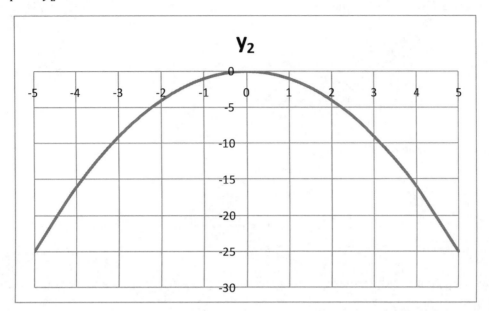

The y values for y_2 are different from those of y_1. Therefore, y_2 has a different range than y_1 and choice B is correct.

46. D: Since the ball drops from 35 feet, the vertex is at (0, 35). Since at 2 seconds after the fall, the height of the ball is 5 feet, the point (2, 5) also satisfies the function. The vertex form of a parabola is $y = a(x - h)^2 + k$ in which (h, k) is the vertex. Substituting in vertex (0, 35) for (h, k) and point (2, 5) for (x, y), $5 = a(2 - 0)^2 + 35$. Then $5 = 2a + 35$, and $a = -15$. The vertex form of this parabola is $y = -15x^2 + 35$ or $h = -15t^2 + 35$. Therefore, choice D is correct.

47. C: The vertex form of a parabola is $y = a(x - h)^2 + k$, in which (h, k) is the vertex. Substituting in the vertex (0, 0) for (h, k) and substituting the point (–2, 8) for (x, y), $8 = a(-2 - 0)^2 + 0$. Then $8 = 4a$, and $a = 2$. The vertex form of this parabola is $y = 2x^2$. Therefore, choice C is correct.

48. C: The vertex form of a parabola is $y = a(x - h)^2 + k$, in which (h, k) is the vertex. Substituting in vertex (–3, –6) for (h, k) and substituting the point (0, 3) for (x, y), $3 = a(0 + 3)^2 - 6$. Then $3 = 9a - 6$, and $a = 1$. The vertex form of this parabola is $y = (x + 3)^2 - 6$. Therefore, choice C is correct.

49. A: The vertex form of a parabola is $y = a(x - h)^2 + k$, in which (h, k) is the vertex. Because we are told that the parabola is symmetrical about the y-axis and that it goes through the point (0, –3), we know that (0, –3) is the vertex. Substituting this point for (h, k) and substituting the point (2, 5) for (x, y), $5 = a(2 - 0)^2 - 3$. Then $8 = 4a$, and $a = 2$. The vertex form of this parabola is $y = 2x^2 - 3$. Therefore, choice A is correct.

50. The correct answer is –5. The x-intercept is determined by setting the equation equal to zero and then solving for x. When $x^2 + 10x + 25 = 0$, then $x = -5$.

51. The correct answer is –2. Because $x^2 = 4$, we can quickly determine that the magnitude of x is 2. The sign, however, alternates between positive and negative. Therefore, x must be –2. Note that multiplying a negative number by itself an even number of times yields a positive number. Multiplying a negative number by itself an odd number of times yields a negative number.

52. The correct answer is –30. The solution is:

$$y = -\frac{1}{6}x$$
$$6y = -x$$
$$-6y = x$$
$$(-6)(5) = x$$
$$-30 = x$$

53. The correct answer is 16. The solution follows:

$$2^x = 65,536$$
$$x\log 2 = \log 65,536$$
$$x = \frac{\log 65,536}{\log 2}$$
$$x = 16$$

54. C: We need to simplify the equation so we can factor it. First, we subtract 2 from each side.

$$3x^2 - 3x - 36 = 0$$

Then we can divide each term by 3.

$$x^2 - x - 12 = 0$$

Finally, we can factor.

$$(x + 3)(x - 4) = 0$$

Setting each factored term equal to 0 yields $x + 3 = 0$ and $x - 4 = 0$, or $x = -3$ and $x = 4$. The sum of –3 and 4 is 1.

55. D: This is an exponential decay function in the form of $y = ab^x$ where $a > 0$ and $0 < b < 1$. Exponential decay functions have domains of all real values or $-\infty \leq x \leq +\infty$, and ranges of all positive real values or $0 < y < +\infty$. Therefore, choice D is correct.

56. C: The equation $y = 3(2)^x$ is an exponential growth function in the form of $y = ab^x$ where $a > 0$ and $b > 1$. An exponential decay function is in the form of $y = ab^x$ where $a > 0$ and $0 < b < 1$. Linear functions only have exponents of 1. Quadratic functions have at least one term of degree 2. Neither linear functions nor quadratic functions have a variable as an exponent. Therefore, choice C is correct.

57. A: For an exponential growth function in the form of $y = ab^x$, $b > 1$. If $b < 1$, the function will decrease instead of increase and correspond to exponential decay rather than exponential growth. It doesn't matter whether a is greater than or less than 1, as long as a is not zero. Therefore, choice A is correct.

58. B: The y-intercept is the point where the graph crosses the y-axis. When giving coordinates for a point, the x-coordinate is given first followed by the y-coordinate. This graph crosses the y-axis at (0, 2). Therefore, choice B is correct.

59. D: The y-intercept of a graph is the point where the graph crosses the x-axis or where $x = 0$. Substituting $x = 0$ into $y = 6\left(\frac{1}{2}\right)^x$ yields $y = 6\left(\frac{1}{2}\right)^0$ or $y = 6$. The y-intercept is $(0, 6)$. Therefore, choice D is correct.

60. C: Use a graphing calculator. Press STAT and select EDIT to enter the year values into List 1. (Use years since 1940: 0, 1, 2, 3, 4.) Enter the population values into List 2. To perform the regression, press STAT and select CALC. Scroll down to ExpReg. Hit ENTER. (Different graphing calculators might involve slightly different procedures; consult the instructions to your calculator.) The particular coefficients may vary slightly, but you should get something like $y = 22{,}245e^{0.0488x}$ or $y = 22{,}245(1.050)^x$. Substituting $x = 10$ (for the year 1950) yields $y = 22{,}245e^{0.0488x} = 36{,}238$

or $y = 22{,}245(1.050)^{10} = 36{,}235$. Therefore, choice C is correct.

Keystone Practice Test #2

1. Let $p(y) = \frac{4y}{2} + 5$. If $y = 4$, then what is the value of $p(y)$?

    a. 9
    b. 7
    c. 13
    d. 37

2. What is the solution to $(3x^2 + 4x - 1) + (2x^2 - 7x - 3)$?

    a. $5x^2 + 3x - 4$
    b. $5x^2 - 3x - 4$
    c. $5x^2 - 3x + 25$
    d. $6x^2 - 11x + 2$

3. What is the solution to $\left(5x^2 - 2x - 2\right) - (3x^2 + 4x - 1)$?

    a. $2x^2 - 6x - 1$
    b. $2x^2 - 6x - 3$
    c. $2x^2 + 2x - 3$
    d. $8x^2 - 6x - 1$

4. Which of the following is equivalent to $3(2x^2 - x - 4)$?

    a. $6x^2 - 3x + 7$
    b. $6x^2 - 3x + 12$
    c. $5x^2 - 3x - 7$
    d. $6x^2 - 3x - 12$

5. Multiply: $(3x - 1)(2x + 5)$.

    a. $6x^2 + 7x + 5$
    b. $6x^2 + 13x + 5$
    c. $6x^2 - 18x - 5$
    d. $6x^2 + 13x - 5$

6. Which of the following binomials can be rewritten as a difference of squares with rational coefficients?

    a. $4x^2 - 20$
    b. $9x^2 - 25$
    c. $6x^2 - 100$
    d. $4x^2 + 25$

7. Which of the following is equivalent to $2\sqrt{4^4}$?

    a. 4
    b. 8
    c. 32
    d. 16

8. Which of the following is equivalent to $(2x^3y)(4x^5y^3)$?

   a. $6x^8y^4$
   b. $8x^8y^4$
   c. $8x^{15}y^3$
   d. $6x^{15}y^3$

9. What is the 7th term of this geometric sequence?

      $-1, 2, -4, 8, \ldots$

   a. 64
   b. -16
   c. -32
   d. -64

10. Which of these graph descriptions fits a relation that is a function?

   a. A vertical line
   b. A parabola that opens to the right
   c. A horizontal line
   d. A circle

11. If $f(x) = 3x^2 - 2x + 3$, what is the value of $f(-2)$?

   a. 11
   b. 19
   c. -5
   d. 21

12. What are the factors of the following polynomial: $x^2 - x - 56$?

   a. $(x - 7)(x + 8)$
   b. $(x + 7)(x - 8)$
   c. $(x - 7)(x - 8)$
   d. $(x + 7)(x + 8)$

13. Which of the following correctly solves the formula $A = \frac{1}{2}(b_1 + b_2)h$ for b_2?

   a. $b_2 = \frac{2A}{hb_1}$
   b. $b_2 = \frac{2h}{A} - b_1$
   c. $b_2 = \frac{2A}{h} - b_1$
   d. $b_2 = \frac{2A}{h} + b_1$

14. Which of the following sets of points describes a function?

   a. $(0,1)(-3,2)(2,-1)(-3,-3)$
   b. $(0,1)(-3,2)(2,1)(-4,7)$
   c. $(0,1)(-3,2)(0,3)(-4,7)$
   d. $(0,1)(-3,2)(-3,1)(2,-1)$

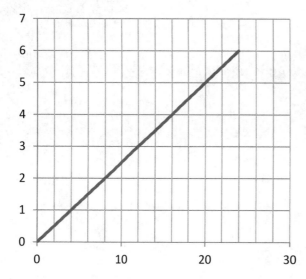

15. What is the slope of a line containing points (−1, 3) and (4, −7)?

   a. $-\dfrac{4}{3}$

   b. −2

   c. $-\dfrac{4}{5}$

   d. 2

16. What is the rate of change represented in this table?

x	y
5	3
10	4
15	5

   a. 3

   b. $\dfrac{1}{3}$

   c. 5

   d. $\dfrac{1}{5}$

17. What is the slope of this line?

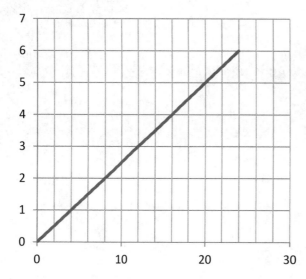

   a. $-\dfrac{1}{4}$

   b. 4

   c. −4

   d. $\dfrac{1}{4}$

18. Julia tracked growth of seedlings over a period of several days and noticed that in a week they grew 10.5 cm. What is the average rate of change?

    a. 10.5 cm /day

    b. 1.5 cm/day

    c. 2.1 cm/day

    d. 2.5 cm/day

19. Which of the following correctly graphs $3x - y < 4$?

    a.

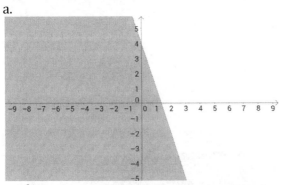

    b.

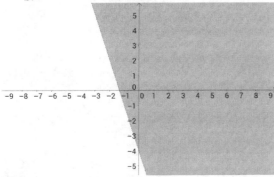

    c.

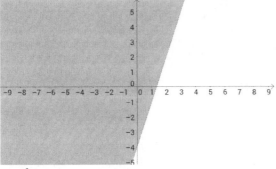

    d.

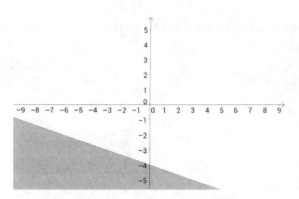

20. **What is the effect on the graph of $f(x) = x$ when $f(x)$ is replaced by $2f(x)$?**

    a. The slope is doubled.
    b. The slope is halved.
    c. The graph is shifted up 2 units.
    d. The graph is shifted down 2 units.

21. **What is the solution to the system of equations represented by the graph below?**

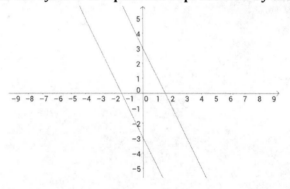

    a. There are an infinite number of solutions.
    b. There is no solution.
    c. $(0, 0)$
    d. $(-3, 3)$

22. Which of the following correctly graphs the system of linear inequalities of $y < 2x + 5$ and $y > x - 3$?

a.

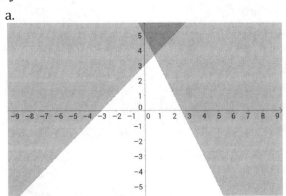

b.

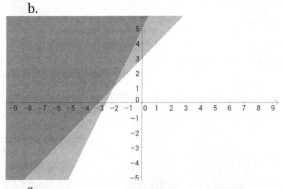

c.

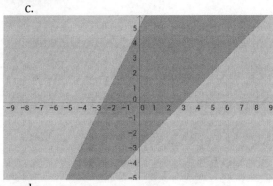

d.

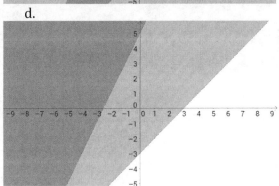

23. Several lab groups perform linear regressions for data sets recorded during a science experiment and calculate the corresponding correlation coefficients. Which lab group's equation for the best-fit line most closely models their data?

Data Set	Correlation coefficient
Steven's lab group	0.823
Sondra's lab group	0.500
Juan's lab group	0.132
Isabella's lab group	0.426

   a. Steven's lab group
   b. Sondra's lab group
   c. Juan's lab group
   d. Isabella's lab group

24. What is the equation of a line that is perpendicular to the y-axis and intersects the point (3,4)?

   a. $y = 4$
   b. $x = 3$
   c. $y = \frac{4}{3}x$
   d. $y = -\frac{3}{4}x + 4$

Question 25 pertains to the following chart:

Beth noticed that the number of questions she answers correctly on a test is directly related to the number of hours she spends studying. The table below lists her scores on five different tests as a function of hours spent studying. Let h represent the number of hours of study and let q represent the number of questions answered correctly.

Number of hours spent studying	Number of questions answered correctly
0.5	65
1	70
1.5	75
2	80
2.5	85

25. If the number of questions Beth answered correctly on a test were written as a linear function of the number of hours she studied, which set of numbers below would represent the domain of that function?

   a. {65, 70, 75, 80, 85}
   b. {0.5, 1, 1.5, 2, 2.5}
   c. {0.5, 65}
   d. {2.5, 85}

Questions 26 and 27 pertain to the following information:

> Will is purchasing notebooks and boxes of pencils for his classroom. He wants to buy a total of 60 items, and he has a total of $100 to purchase the items. Notebooks cost $1.50 each and pencils cost $2 per box. Let N represent the number of notebooks and let P represent the number of boxes of pencils Will is going to purchase.

26. Which system of linear equations can be used to solve for the number of notebooks and pencils Will plans to purchase?

a. $\begin{cases} 1.5N + 2P = 60 \\ N + P = 100 \end{cases}$

b. $\begin{cases} N + P = 60 \\ 1.5N + 2P = 100 \end{cases}$

c. $\begin{cases} N + P = 60 \\ 2N + 1.5P = 100 \end{cases}$

d. $\begin{cases} 2N + 1.5P = 60 \\ 1.5N + 2P = 100 \end{cases}$

27. How many notebooks is Will planning to buy?

a. 15
b. 20
c. 40
d. 55

28. Which of the following is the value of x when $-3x + 1 < 2$?

a. $x < \dfrac{1}{3}$

b. $x > \dfrac{1}{3}$

c. $x < -\dfrac{1}{3}$

d. $x > -\dfrac{1}{3}$

29. The table shows the number of students enrolled in an afterschool taekwondo program by age groups.

Age	7	8	9	10
Enrollees in taekwondo	18	15	11	8

Which of the following equations represents the best-fit line for these data?

a. $y = -3.1x + 43.7$
b. $y = -3.4x + 41.9$
c. $y = -3.7x + 39.5$
d. $y = -3.9x + 37.3$

30. A study found a correlation coefficient of –0.143 between consumption of watermelon and heart disease. Which of the following conclusions can be drawn from these data?

a. Eating watermelon causes heart disease.
b. Eating watermelon helps prevent heart disease.
c. Eating watermelon is associated with a higher rate of heart disease.
d. Eating watermelon is not associated with a higher rate of heart disease.

31. The table shows the number of minutes a student practiced the violin the first four weeks of lessons. Based on these data, approximately how many minutes will the student practice week 7?

Week	1	2	3	4
Minutes practiced	20	37	49	55

    a. 89 minutes
    b. 91 minutes
    c. 92 minutes
    d. 93 minutes

32. What are the domain and range of the function represented by this table?

x	y
3	−3
−2	9
10	0
−5	4
7	−10

    a. The domain is {−10, −5, −3, −2, 0}, and the range is {3, 4, 7, 9, 10}.
    b. The domain is {3, 4, 7, 9, 10}, and the range is {−10, −5, −3, −2, 0}.
    c. The domain is {−5, −2, 3, 7, 10}, and the range is {−10, −3, 0, 4, 9}.
    d. The domain is {−10, −3, 0, 4, 9}, and the range is {−5, −2, 3, 7, 10}.

33. Which of the following is the equation for the line containing points (−3, −1) and (7, −2)?

    a. $y = -\frac{3}{10}x + \frac{13}{10}$
    b. $y = -\frac{1}{10}x - \frac{13}{10}$
    c. $y = \frac{1}{10}x - \frac{7}{10}$
    d. $y = -\frac{1}{10}x + \frac{13}{10}$

34. Which of the following is the linear equation representing the function given by this table?

x	y
−5	1
−4	3
−3	5
−2	7
−1	9

    a. $y = -2x - 9$
    b. $y = 2x + 11$
    c. $y = 2x - 11$
    d. $y = -2x + 9$

35. Which of the following equations is represented by this graph?

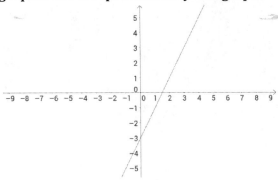

    a. $y = 2x - 3$
    b. $y = 3x - 3$
    c. $y = x - 2$
    d. $y = 2x - 5$

36. Given that y varies directly as x, if $y = 6$ when $x = 3$, which of these equations relates x to y?

    a. $y = 2x$
    b. $y = 6x$
    c. $y = 3x$
    d. $y = 9x$

37. Which of these equations represents a line that passes through point (–2, 1) and is parallel to $y = 3x - 1$?

    a. $y = x - 2$
    b. $y = -2x - 1$
    c. $y = 3x + 7$
    d. $y = 3x + 5$

38. Which of these equations represents a line that passes through point (3, –6) and that is perpendicular to $y = 4x + 3$?

    a. $y = -4x - 6$
    b. $y = -4x + 6$
    c. $y = \dfrac{x}{4} - \dfrac{27}{4}$
    d. $y = -\dfrac{x}{4} - \dfrac{21}{4}$

39. Which of the following is the equation for the line with a slope of –3 that passes through point (–1, 5)?

    a. $y = 5x - 4$
    b. $y = -x + 5$
    c. $y = -3x + 2$
    d. $y = -3x + 1$

40. What is the domain and the range of this function?

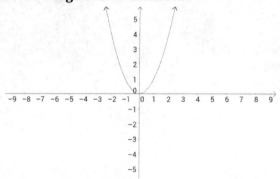

a. The domain is $x \leq 0$, and the range is $y \geq 0$.
b. The domain is $-\infty \leq x \leq +\infty$, and the range is $-\infty \leq y \leq +\infty$.
c. The domain is $x \geq 0$ and the range is $-\infty \leq y \leq +\infty$.
d. The domain is $-\infty \leq x \leq +\infty$, and the range is $y \geq 0$.

41. What are the domain and range of the equation graphed below?

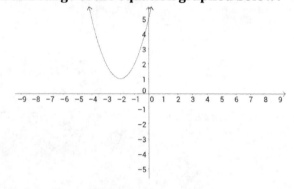

a. The domain is $-10 \leq x \leq +10$, and the range is $y \geq 1$.
b. The domain is $-\infty \leq x \leq +\infty$, and the range is $y \geq 1$.
c. The domain is $-10 \leq x \leq +10$, and the range is $y \geq 0$.
d. The domain is $-\infty \leq x \leq +\infty$, and the range is $y \geq 0$.

42. Match the following graphs to their respective functions: y_1, y_2, and y_3.

$y_1 = x^2$
$y_2 = -x^2$
$y_3 = x^2 + 10$

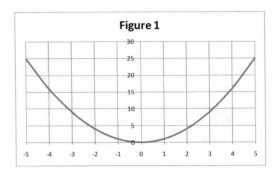

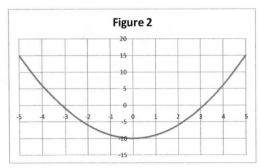

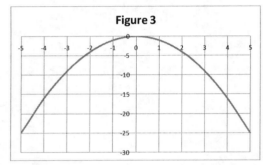

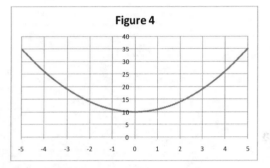

    a.   Figure 1 contains y_1. Figure 2 contains y_2. Figure 3 contains y_3.
    b.   Figure 2 contains y_1. Figure 3 contains y_2. Figure 4 contains y_3.
    c.   Figure 1 contains y_1. Figure 3 contains y_2. Figure 4 contains y_3.
    d.   Figure 3 contains y_1. Figure 2 contains y_2. Figure 1 contains y_3.

43. What is the y-intercept of the line described by Equation A: $5y - 100x = 25$? Write your answer in the answer grid.

-	0	0
+	1	1
	2	2
	3	3
	4	4
	5	5
	6	6
	7	7
	8	8
	9	9

44. Solve for A: $\frac{6+A}{5} = -2$ and write your answer in the answer grid.

-	0	0
+	1	1
	2	2
	3	3
	4	4
	5	5
	6	6
	7	7
	8	8
	9	9

45. Solve the following equation for x, and write your answer in the answer grid.

$$x^2 + 10x = -25$$

-	0	0
+	1	1
	2	2
	3	3
	4	4
	5	5
	6	6
	7	7
	8	8
	9	9

46. The axis of symmetry of this parabola is $x =$ _____ (write your answer in the answer grid).

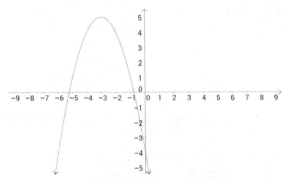

-	0	0
+	1	1
	2	2
	3	3
	4	4
	5	5
	6	6
	7	7
	8	8
	9	9

47. What is the sum of all values of x that satisfy the following equation?

$$5x^2 - 30x - 32 = 3$$

   a. -1
   b. 0
   c. 6
   d. 7

48. Which of the following equations is equivalent to $y = 3(x - 1)^2 + 4$?

   a. $y = 3x^2 - 6x + 7$
   b. $y = 3x^2 - 2x + 7$
   c. $y = 3x^2 + 6x + 4$
   d. $y = 2x^2 - 5x + 4$

49. Which of the following equations is equivalent to $y = -2(x + 5)^2 - 8$?

   a. $y = 2x^2 + 20x + 42$
   b. $y = -2x^2 + 20x + 42$
   c. $y = -2x^2 - 20x - 50$
   d. $y = -2x^2 - 20x - 58$

50. A rock falls from a 50-foot cliff. The height (h) in feet of the rock is modeled as a quadratic function of time (t) in seconds. If the rock is at 34 feet at 1 second after the fall, which of these functions represents this situation?

    a. $h = -84t^2 + 50$
    b. $h = -34t^2 + 50$
    c. $h = 84t^2 + 50$
    d. $h = -16t^2 + 50$

51. Which of the following statements is true regarding the linear factors of a quadratic equation?

    a. The zeros of the quadratic equation can be determined directly from the linear factors.
    b. The vertex of the quadratic equation can be determined directly from the linear factors.
    c. The axis of symmetry of the quadratic equation can be determined directly from the linear factors.
    d. The y-intercept of the quadratic equation can be determined directly from the linear factors.

52. What are the zeros of this quadratic function?

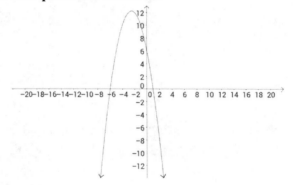

    a. $-2, 16$
    b. $-6, 1$
    c. $0, 12$
    d. $-2, 2$

53. What is the solution to $2x^2 - x - 5 = 0$?

    a. $x = \dfrac{1 \pm \sqrt{-39}}{4}$
    b. $x = \dfrac{1 \pm \sqrt{-41}}{2}$
    c. $x = \dfrac{1 \pm \sqrt{41}}{4}$
    d. $x = \dfrac{-1 \pm \sqrt{39}}{4}$

54. What are the domain and range of $y = 2^x$?

    a. The domain is $-2 \leq x$, and the range is $y < 2$.
    b. The domain is $-\infty < x < +\infty$, and the range is $-2 < y < +\infty$.
    c. The domain is $0 < x \leq +\infty$, and the range is $-\infty < y < +\infty$.
    d. The domain is $-\infty < x < +\infty$, and the range is $0 < y < +\infty$.

55. What is the range of the exponential decay function pictured below?

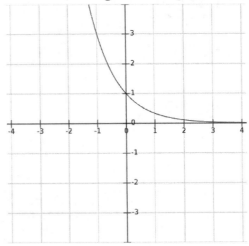

a. $-\infty < y < +\infty$
b. $0 < y < +\infty$
c. $-2 < y < +\infty$
d. $-\infty < x < +\infty$

56. Which of the following statements is true regarding the equation $y = 5\left(\frac{1}{4}\right)^x$?

a. This is an exponential decay function.
b. This is a linear function.
c. This is an exponential growth function.
d. This is a quadratic function.

57. Which of the following exponential functions models the growth of a town with a population of 20,000 with an annual increase of 2%?

a. $y = 20,001.02^x$
b. $y = 20,000(x)^{1.02}$
c. $y = 20,000(1.02)^x$
d. $y = 20,000(.02)^x$

58. Which of the following exponential functions models the growth of a $500 investment that is compounded annually with an interest rate of 4%?

a. $y = 500(4)^x$
b. $y = 500(x)^{1.04}$
c. $y = 5(400)^x$
d. $y = 500(1.04)^x$

59. Which of the following exponential functions models the decay in value of a $40,000 truck that loses 10% of its value every year?

a. $y = 500(4)^x$
b. $y = 40,000(0.90)^x$
c. $y = 5(400)^x$
d. $y = 500(1.04)^x$

60. Which of the following exponential functions provides a reasonable fit to this data?

x	y
0	57.2
5	28.5
10	14.2
15	7.08
20	3.52

a. $y = 57.22(0.870)^x$
b. $y = 56.99(0.560)^x$
c. $y = 3.52(0.615)^x$
d. $y = 28.5(5)^x$

Answer Key and Explanations for Test #2

1. C: The equation describes a functional relationship between y and $p(y)$. To solve the equation, substitute 4 as the value of y, such that

$$p(4) = \frac{4(4)}{2} + 5 = \frac{16}{2} + 5 = 8 + 5 = 13.$$

Therefore, choice C is correct.

2. B: When adding these polynomials, the parentheses can simply be removed, which results in $3x^2 + 4x - 1 + 2x^2 - 7x - 3$. Collecting like terms yields $5x^2 - 3x - 4$. Therefore, choice B is correct.

3. A: When subtracting polynomials, the parentheses around the first polynomial can simply be removed. When removing the parentheses around the second polynomial, the sign of each term must be switched. This results in $5x^2 - 2x - 2 - 3x^2 - 4x + 1$. Collecting like terms yields $2x^2 - 6x - 1$. Therefore, choice A is correct.

4. D: Applying the distributive property results in $3 \cdot 2x^2 - 3 \cdot x - 3 \cdot 4$. This expression can be simplified to $6x^2 - 3x - 12$. Therefore, choice D is correct.

5. D: Multiply each term in one set of parentheses by each term in the other set: $(3x)(2x) + (3x)(5) + (-1)(2x) + (-1)(5) = 6x^2 + 15x - 2x - 5$. Then combine like terms: $6x^2 + 13x - 5$. Therefore, choice D is correct.

6. B: A difference of squares factors to a sum and a difference. For example, $a^2 - b^2$ factors to $(a + b)(a - b)$. The binomial $9x^2 - 25$ can be rewritten as $(3x)^2 - (5)^2$. Then $(3x)^2 - (5)^2$ can be factored to $(3x + 5)(3x - 5)$. Therefore, choice B is correct.

7. C: The radical $2\sqrt{4^4}$ can be written as $2 \cdot 4^{\frac{4}{2}}$ which is equal to $2 \cdot 4^2$ or $2 \cdot 16$ or 32. Therefore, choice C is correct.

8. B: When multiplying expressions with exponents, the exponents of the like bases are added. The coefficients of the expressions are multiplied. For the problem $(2x^3y)(4x^5y^3)$, the product is $8x^8y^4$. Therefore, choice B is correct.

9. D: Consecutive terms in a geometric sequence have a common ratio. The common ratio of this sequence is –2. The next three terms are –16, 32, and –64. The 7th term is –64. Therefore, choice D is correct.

10. C: A function is a relation that has only one output for each input or only one y-value for each x-value. A vertical line drawn anywhere over the graph of a function will intersect the function at one point at most. Of the given choices, only a horizontal line fits this description. Each x-value of a horizontal line has only one y-value. Therefore, choice C is correct.

11. B: To solve, substitute $x = -2$ into $f(x) = 3x^2 - 2x + 3$. So $f(-2) = 3(-2)^2 - 2(-2) + 3 = 12 + 4 + 3 = 19$. Therefore, choice B is correct.

12. B: To factor the polynomial, find factors of the first and third term whose product can be added to get the middle term. Here, the factors 7 and –8 have a product of –56, and when added together

129

yield –1. Another way to find the correct answer is to multiply the answer choices and select the choice that yields the original equation. In this case:

$$(x + 7)(x - 8) = (x)(x) + (x)(-8) + (7)(x) + (7)(-8)$$
$$= x^2 - 8x + 7x - 56$$
$$= x^2 - x - 56$$

Therefore, choice B is correct.

13. C: Multiplying both sides by 2 yields $2A = (b_1 + b_2)h$. Then dividing both sides by h yields $\frac{2A}{h} = b_1 + b_2$. Finally, subtracting b_1 from both sides yields $b_2 = \frac{2A}{h} - b_1$. Therefore, choice C is correct.

14. B: A function has exactly one y-value for each x-value. Choices A, C, and D each have x-values with multiple y-values. Therefore, choice B is correct.

15. B: The slope can be found from $m = \frac{y_2 - y_1}{x_2 - x_1}$. Substituting the x-values and y-values from the given points yields $m = \frac{-7-3}{4-(-1)} = \frac{-10}{5} = -2$. The slope is –2. Therefore, choice B is correct.

16. D: The slope can be found from $m = \frac{y_2 - y_1}{x_2 - x_1}$. Substituting the x-values and y-values from the first two rows of the table yields $m = \frac{4-3}{10-5} = \frac{1}{5}$. The slope is $\frac{1}{5}$. Therefore, choice D is correct.

17. D: The slope is the change in y over the change in x, or the slope can be found from $m = \frac{y_2 - y_1}{x_2 - x_1}$. Since the line slants up to the right, the slope is positive. Selecting the points located at (12, 3) and (0, 0) and substituting the x-values and y-values into the formula yields $m = \frac{3-0}{12-0} = \frac{3}{12}$ or $\frac{1}{4}$. The slope is $\frac{1}{4}$. Therefore, choice D is correct. (Note that we didn't have to choose those two specific points; choosing any two points on the line would have resulted in the same answer.) Therefore, choice D is correct.

18. B: Rate of change, or slope, is calculated by dividing total change by total time. The seedlings grew 10.5 cm in 7 days, so the average rate of change is 10.5 ÷ 7, or 1.5 cm per day. Therefore, choice B is correct.

19. C: First, solving $3x - y < 4$ for y results in $y > 3x - 4$. Then graph a dashed line with slope of 3 and y-intercept of –4. Select (0, 0) as a test point. Check if $0 > 3(0) - 4$. Since this statement is true, shade the side of the line containing the point (0, 0). Therefore, choice C is correct.

20. B: The effect on the graph of $f(x) = x$ when $f(x)$ is replaced by $2f(x)$ is that the slope is halved. Solving the equation $2f(x) = x$ for $f(x)$ yields $f(x) = \frac{x}{2}$. The slope of the line changes from 1 to $\frac{1}{2}$. Therefore, choice B is correct.

21. B: This system is of parallel lines. Since the lines never intersect, there is no solution. Therefore, choice B is correct.

22. C: First, graph a dashed line for $y = 2x + 5$. Using (0, 0) as a test point, check if $0 = 2(0) + 5$. Since it's a true statement, shade the side of line $y = 2x + 5$ that includes (0, 0). Then, graph a dashed line for $y = x - 3$. Using (0, 0) as a test point, check if $0 > 0 - 3$. Since it's a true statement, shade the side of the line $y = x - 3$ that includes (0, 0). The area where the two shaded regions overlap is the solution to this system of inequalities. Therefore, choice C is correct.

23. A: The graphing calculator determines the best-fit line during the linear regression. The correlation coefficient measures how closely the equation of that best-fit line models the data. The closer the correlation coefficient is to 1 or –1, the better the model. Since Steven's lab group calculated a correlation coefficient of 0.823, which is the closest to 1, his lab group has the best model. Therefore, choice A is correct.

24. A: A line that is perpendicular to the y-axis is horizontal, with a slope of 0. Because it passes through the point (3, 4), we know that the y-value for the entire line is 4, and thus the equation is $y = 4$. Therefore, choice A is correct.

25. B: The domain consists of all the values of the independent variable. In this case, the independent variable is the number of hours spent studying. Therefore, choice B is correct.

26. B: Since Will is buying a total of 60 items, the number of notebooks plus the number of boxes of pencils is 60 or $N + P = 60$. Each notebook costs $1.50, so multiply the number of notebooks by 1.5. Each box of pencils costs $2, so multiply the number of boxes by 2. Will has a total of $100 to spend, so $1.5N + 2P = 100$. Therefore, choice B is correct.

27. C: Use a linear system of equations to find the number of notebooks. See the explanation for question 24. In this case, the system of equations is $N + P = 60$ and $1.5N + 2P = 100$. Begin with $N + P = 60$ and solve for P.

$$N + P = 60$$
$$P = 60 - N$$

Now substitute the equation for P into the equation $1.5N + 2P = 100$:

$$1.5N + 2P = 100$$
$$1.5N + 2(60 - N) = 100$$
$$1.5N + 120 - 2N = 100$$
$$-0.5N = -20$$
$$N = 40$$

Will is going to buy 40 notebooks. Therefore, choice C is correct.

28. D: To solve, we first subtract 1 from each side: $-3x < 2 - 1 \rightarrow -3x < 1$. Then divide each side by –3 (note that changing the sign involves flipping the inequality): $x > -\frac{1}{3}$. To test, we can choose any number greater than $-\frac{1}{3}$, such as 0, and substitute for x in the original equation: $-3(0) + 1 < 2 \rightarrow 1 < 2$. This is true, so the equation seems to be true. We can further test by choosing a number outside the range, such as –1: $-3(-1) + 1 < 2 \rightarrow 4 < 2$. Since 4 is not less than 2, this is not true, further verifying the answer. Therefore, choice D is correct.

29. B: Use a graphing calculator. Press STAT and select EDIT to enter the *Age* data into List 1. Enter the *Enrollees in taekwondo* data into List 2. To perform the regression, press STAT and select CALC. Scroll down to LinReg($ax+b$). (Different graphing calculators might involve slightly different procedures; consult the instructions to your calculator.) With an equation in the form of $y = ax + b$, $a = -3.4$ and $b = 41.9$. Then the equation is $y = -3.4x + 41.9$. Therefore, choice B is correct.

30. D: Since the correlation coefficient is close to 0, there is a very weak negative correlation between the variables. Because correlation does not imply causation, the first two choices cannot

131

be correct. Eating watermelon does not appear to have an association with rates of heart disease, due to the weak correlation. Therefore, choice D is correct.

31. D: Use a graphing calculator. Press STAT and select EDIT to enter the *Week* data into List 1. Enter the *Minutes practiced* data into List 2. To perform the regression, press STAT and select CALC. Scroll down to LinReg($ax+b$). (Different graphing calculators might involve slightly different procedures; consult the instructions to your calculator.) With an equation in the form of $y = ax + b$, a = 11.7 and b = 11. The equation is $y = 11.7x + 11$. If $x = 7$, $y = (11.7)(7) + 11$ or approximately 93 minutes. Therefore, choice D is correct.

32. C: The domain is the set containing all of the inputs or x-values for the function. The range is the set containing all of the outputs or y-values for the function. The domain is $\{-5, -2, 3, 7, 10\}$, and the range is $\{-10, -3, 0, 4, 9\}$. Therefore, choice C is correct.

33. B: The slope can be found from $m = \frac{y_2 - y_1}{x_2 - x_1}$. Then $m = \frac{-2 - (-1)}{7 - (-3)} = \frac{-2 + 1}{7 + 3} = -\frac{1}{10}$. Substituting point $(-3, -1)$ and this slope into $y = mx + b$ yields $-1 = \left(-\frac{1}{10}\right)(-3) + b$. Solving for b, $b = -1 - \frac{3}{10} = -\frac{13}{10}$. The equation of this line is $y = -\frac{1}{10}x - \frac{13}{10}$. Therefore, choice B is correct.

34. B: The slope is the change in y-values over the change in x-values. The change in y-values between successive rows is +2. The change in x-values is +1. Thus the slope is $\frac{+2}{+1}$ or 2. Then plugging the first row into $y = mx + b$ yields $1 = 2(-5) + b$ or $1 = -10 + b$. Then, $b = 11$. The equation is $y = 2x + 11$. Therefore, choice B is correct.

35. A: The slope and the y-intercept can be read from the graph. The y-intercept is -3. The slope is 2. The equation of this line is $y = 2x - 3$. Therefore, choice A is correct.

36. A: Substituting $y = 6$ and $x = 3$ into $y = kx$ yields $6 = k(3)$ which means $k = 2$. The equation for this direct variation is $y = 2x$. Therefore, choice A is correct.

37. C: Parallel lines have the same slope. Since the slope of $y = 3x - 1$ is 3, the slope of the parallel line is also 3. The equation can be found by plugging the slope and point into the formula $y - y_1 = m(x - x_1)$. Then, $y - 1 = 3(x + 2)$. Rearranging yields $y - 1 = 3x + 6$ or $y = 3x + 7$. Therefore, choice C is correct.

38. D: The slopes of perpendicular lines are negative multiplicative inverses or negative reciprocals. Since the slope of $y = 4x + 3$ is 4, the slope of a line perpendicular to it is $-\frac{1}{4}$. The equation of the line can be found by plugging the slope and point into the formula $y - y_1 = m(x - x_1)$. Then, $y + 6 = -\frac{1}{4}(x - 3)$ or $y + 6 = -\frac{x}{4} + \frac{3}{4}$. Finally, $y = -\frac{x}{4} - \frac{21}{4}$. Therefore, choice D is correct.

39. C: The slope and the point can be substituted into the formula $y - y_1 = m(x - x_1)$. Then $y - 5 = -3(x + 1)$. Rearranging yields $y - 5 = -3x - 3$ or $y = -3x + 2$. Therefore, choice C is correct.

40. D: The domain is all of the x-values for the function. The range is all y-values for the function. This function includes all real x-values, but y is always non-negative. The domain is $-\infty \leq x \leq +\infty$, and the range is $y \geq 0$. Therefore, choice D is correct.

41. B: The domain is all of the x-values for the function. The range is all y-values for the function. This function includes all real x-values, but the minimum y-value is 1. The domain is $-\infty \leq x \leq +\infty$, and the range is $y \geq 1$. Therefore, choice B is correct.

42. C: The graph of y_1 matches Figure 1. The graph opens up, with the vertex at $(0,0)$, so it is the parent function of $y = x^2$. Figure 3 opens downward with the vertex at $(0,0)$, so it is simply the parent function flipped: $y = -x^2$. Figure 4 opens upward with the vertex at $(0,10)$, so it shifts the parent function up by 10: $y = x^2 + 10$. Figure 2 is not represented. It opens upward with the vertex at $(0,-10)$, so the parent function is shifted down 10: $y = x^2 - 10$. Therefore, choice C is correct.

43. The correct answer is 5. First write Equation A in slope-intercept form: $y = mx + b$ where m is the slope and b is the y-intercept.

$$5y - 100x = 25$$
$$5y = 100x + 25$$
$$y = 20x + 5$$

Based on the slope-intercept form of Equation A, the y-intercept is $b = 5$.

44. The correct answer is −16. To solve for A, we first need to multiply each side by 5: $6 + A = (-2)(5) \rightarrow 6 + A = -10$. Then subtract 6 from each side to find that $A = -16$.

45. The correct answer is −5. The solution follows:
$$x^2 + 10x = -25$$
$$x^2 + 10x + 25 = 0$$
$$(x + 5)(x + 5) = 0$$
$$x = -5$$

46. The correct answer is −3. The axis of symmetry is the central line about which the parabola is symmetric. The vertex is the point at which the parabola intersects the axis of symmetry (which is also the parabola's maximum or minimum point). The equation of the axis of symmetry is $x = -3$.

47. C: We need to simplify the equation so we can factor it. First, we subtract 3 from each side.

$$5x^2 - 30x - 35 = 0$$

Then we can divide each term by 5.

$$x^2 - 6x - 7 = 0$$

Finally, we can factor.

$$(x + 1)(x - 7) = 0$$

Setting each factored term equal to 0 yields $x + 1 = 0$ and $x - 7 = 0$, or $x = -1$ and $x = 7$. The sum of −1 and 7 is 6.

48. A: The equation of the parabola $y = 3(x - 1)^2 + 4$ is in vertex form. This can be expanded to $y = 3(x^2 - 2x + 1) + 4$ or $y = 3x^2 - 6x + 3 + 4$. Finally, this can be written as $y = 3x^2 - 6x + 7$. Therefore, choice A is correct.

49. D: The equation of the parabola $y = -2(x + 5)^2 - 8$ is in vertex form. This can be expanded to $y = -2(x^2 + 10x + 25) - 8$ or $y = -2x^2 - 20x - 50 - 8$. Finally, this can be written as $y = -2x^2 - 20x - 58$. Therefore, choice D is correct.

50. D: Since the rock drops from a 50-foot cliff, the vertex is at $(0, 50)$. Since at 1 second after the fall, the height of the rock is 34 feet, the point $(1, 34)$ also satisfies the function. The vertex form of a parabola is $y = a(x - h)^2 + k$ in which (h, k) is the vertex. Substituting in vertex $(0, 50)$ for (h, k) and point $(1, 34)$ for (x, y), $34 = a(1 - 0)^2 + 50$. Then $34 = a + 50$, and $a = -16$. The vertex form of this parabola is $y = -16x^2 + 50$ or $h = -16t^2 + 50$. Therefore, choice D is correct.

51. A: The zeros are the x-values for which the equation equals zero. If a quadratic equation can be factored, the zeros can be determined directly from the linear factors, by setting each factor equal to zero. Therefore, choice A is correct.

52. B: The zeros are the x-values where the graph of the quadratic equation crosses the x-axis. The graph crosses the x-axis at $(-6, 0)$ and $(1, 0)$. The zeros are -6 and 1. Therefore, choice B is correct.

53. C: This can be solved using the quadratic formula $x = \frac{-b \pm \sqrt{b^2 - 4ac}}{2a}$. Then, $x = \frac{-(-1) \pm \sqrt{(-1)^2 - 4(2)(-5)}}{2(2)}$. Simplifying, $x = \frac{1 \pm \sqrt{41}}{4}$. Therefore, choice C is correct.

54. D: This is an exponential growth function in the form of $y = ab^x$ where $a > 0$ and $b > 1$. Exponential growth functions have domains of all real values or $-\infty < x < +\infty$, and ranges of all positive real values or $0 < y < +\infty$. Therefore, choice D is correct.

55. B: This is an exponential decay function in the form of $y = ab^x$ where $a > 0$ and $0 < b < 1$. Exponential decay functions have domains of all real values or $-\infty \leq x \leq +\infty$, and ranges of all positive real values or $0 < y < +\infty$. Therefore, choice B is correct.

56. A: The equation is an exponential decay function in the form of $y = ab^x$ where $a > 0$ and $0 < b < 1$. Linear functions only have exponents of 1. Quadratic functions have at least one term of degree 2. Neither linear functions nor quadratic functions have a variable as an exponent. An exponential growth function is in the form of $y = ab^x$ where $a > 0$ and $b > 1$. Therefore, choice A is correct.

57. C: This is an exponential growth function in the form of $y = ab^x$. In this equation, a is the initial value, which is given here as 20,000, and b is the growth rate. An annual increase of 2% means a rate of growth of 102%, or 1.02. Then, $y = 20,000(1.02)^x$. Therefore, choice C is correct.

58. D: This is an exponential growth function in the form of $y = ab^x$. In this equation, a is the initial value, which is given here as 500, and b is the growth rate. An interest rate of 4% means a rate of growth of 104%, or 1.04. Then, $y = 500(1.04)^x$. Therefore, choice D is correct.

59. B: The equation is an exponential decay function in the form of $y = ab^x$ where $a > 0$ and $0 < b < 1$. Since the truck loses 10% of its value every year, each year its value is 90% of the previous year. That means $b = 0.90$. The starting value, or a, is given here as 40,000. The equation is $y = 40,000(0.90)^x$. Therefore, choice B is correct.

60. A: Use a graphing calculator. Press STAT and select EDIT to enter the x-values into List 1. Enter the y-values into List 2. To perform the regression, press STAT and select CALC. Scroll down to ExpReg. Hit ENTER. (Different graphing calculators might involve slightly different procedures; consult the instructions to your calculator.) The equation is $y = 57.22(0.870)^x$. Therefore, choice A is correct.

How to Overcome Test Anxiety

Just the thought of taking a test is enough to make most people a little nervous. A test is an important event that can have a long-term impact on your future, so it's important to take it seriously and it's natural to feel anxious about performing well. But just because anxiety is normal, that doesn't mean that it's helpful in test taking, or that you should simply accept it as part of your life. Anxiety can have a variety of effects. These effects can be mild, like making you feel slightly nervous, or severe, like blocking your ability to focus or remember even a simple detail.

If you experience test anxiety—whether severe or mild—it's important to know how to beat it. To discover this, first you need to understand what causes test anxiety.

Causes of Test Anxiety

While we often think of anxiety as an uncontrollable emotional state, it can actually be caused by simple, practical things. One of the most common causes of test anxiety is that a person does not feel adequately prepared for their test. This feeling can be the result of many different issues such as poor study habits or lack of organization, but the most common culprit is time management. Starting to study too late, failing to organize your study time to cover all of the material, or being distracted while you study will mean that you're not well prepared for the test. This may lead to cramming the night before, which will cause you to be physically and mentally exhausted for the test. Poor time management also contributes to feelings of stress, fear, and hopelessness as you realize you are not well prepared but don't know what to do about it.

Other times, test anxiety is not related to your preparation for the test but comes from unresolved fear. This may be a past failure on a test, or poor performance on tests in general. It may come from comparing yourself to others who seem to be performing better or from the stress of living up to expectations. Anxiety may be driven by fears of the future—how failure on this test would affect your educational and career goals. These fears are often completely irrational, but they can still negatively impact your test performance.

Elements of Test Anxiety

As mentioned earlier, test anxiety is considered to be an emotional state, but it has physical and mental components as well. Sometimes you may not even realize that you are suffering from test anxiety until you notice the physical symptoms. These can include trembling hands, rapid heartbeat, sweating, nausea, and tense muscles. Extreme anxiety may lead to fainting or vomiting. Obviously, any of these symptoms can have a negative impact on testing. It is important to recognize them as soon as they begin to occur so that you can address the problem before it damages your performance.

The mental components of test anxiety include trouble focusing and inability to remember learned information. During a test, your mind is on high alert, which can help you recall information and stay focused for an extended period of time. However, anxiety interferes with your mind's natural processes, causing you to blank out, even on the questions you know well. The strain of testing during anxiety makes it difficult to stay focused, especially on a test that may take several hours. Extreme anxiety can take a huge mental toll, making it difficult not only to recall test information but even to understand the test questions or pull your thoughts together.

135

Effects of Test Anxiety

Test anxiety is like a disease—if left untreated, it will get progressively worse. Anxiety leads to poor performance, and this reinforces the feelings of fear and failure, which in turn lead to poor performances on subsequent tests. It can grow from a mild nervousness to a crippling condition. If allowed to progress, test anxiety can have a big impact on your schooling, and consequently on your future.

Test anxiety can spread to other parts of your life. Anxiety on tests can become anxiety in any stressful situation, and blanking on a test can turn into panicking in a job situation. But fortunately, you don't have to let anxiety rule your testing and determine your grades. There are a number of relatively simple steps you can take to move past anxiety and function normally on a test and in the rest of life.

Physical Steps for Beating Test Anxiety

While test anxiety is a serious problem, the good news is that it can be overcome. It doesn't have to control your ability to think and remember information. While it may take time, you can begin taking steps today to beat anxiety.

Just as your first hint that you may be struggling with anxiety comes from the physical symptoms, the first step to treating it is also physical. Rest is crucial for having a clear, strong mind. If you are tired, it is much easier to give in to anxiety. But if you establish good sleep habits, your body and mind will be ready to perform optimally, without the strain of exhaustion. Additionally, sleeping well helps you to retain information better, so you're more likely to recall the answers when you see the test questions.

Getting good sleep means more than going to bed on time. It's important to allow your brain time to relax. Take study breaks from time to time so it doesn't get overworked, and don't study right before bed. Take time to rest your mind before trying to rest your body, or you may find it difficult to fall asleep.

Along with sleep, other aspects of physical health are important in preparing for a test. Good nutrition is vital for good brain function. Sugary foods and drinks may give a burst of energy but this burst is followed by a crash, both physically and emotionally. Instead, fuel your body with protein and vitamin-rich foods.

Also, drink plenty of water. Dehydration can lead to headaches and exhaustion, especially if your brain is already under stress from the rigors of the test. Particularly if your test is a long one, drink water during the breaks. And if possible, take an energy-boosting snack to eat between sections.

Along with sleep and diet, a third important part of physical health is exercise. Maintaining a steady workout schedule is helpful, but even taking 5-minute study breaks to walk can help get your blood pumping faster and clear your head. Exercise also releases endorphins, which contribute to a positive feeling and can help combat test anxiety.

When you nurture your physical health, you are also contributing to your mental health. If your body is healthy, your mind is much more likely to be healthy as well. So take time to rest, nourish your body with healthy food and water, and get moving as much as possible. Taking these physical steps will make you stronger and more able to take the mental steps necessary to overcome test anxiety.

Mental Steps for Beating Test Anxiety

Working on the mental side of test anxiety can be more challenging, but as with the physical side, there are clear steps you can take to overcome it. As mentioned earlier, test anxiety often stems from lack of preparation, so the obvious solution is to prepare for the test. Effective studying may be the most important weapon you have for beating test anxiety, but you can and should employ several other mental tools to combat fear.

First, boost your confidence by reminding yourself of past success—tests or projects that you aced. If you're putting as much effort into preparing for this test as you did for those, there's no reason you should expect to fail here. Work hard to prepare; then trust your preparation.

Second, surround yourself with encouraging people. It can be helpful to find a study group, but be sure that the people you're around will encourage a positive attitude. If you spend time with others who are anxious or cynical, this will only contribute to your own anxiety. Look for others who are motivated to study hard from a desire to succeed, not from a fear of failure.

Third, reward yourself. A test is physically and mentally tiring, even without anxiety, and it can be helpful to have something to look forward to. Plan an activity following the test, regardless of the outcome, such as going to a movie or getting ice cream.

When you are taking the test, if you find yourself beginning to feel anxious, remind yourself that you know the material. Visualize successfully completing the test. Then take a few deep, relaxing breaths and return to it. Work through the questions carefully but with confidence, knowing that you are capable of succeeding.

Developing a healthy mental approach to test taking will also aid in other areas of life. Test anxiety affects more than just the actual test—it can be damaging to your mental health and even contribute to depression. It's important to beat test anxiety before it becomes a problem for more than testing.

Study Strategy

Being prepared for the test is necessary to combat anxiety, but what does being prepared look like? You may study for hours on end and still not feel prepared. What you need is a strategy for test prep. The next few pages outline our recommended steps to help you plan out and conquer the challenge of preparation.

STEP 1: SCOPE OUT THE TEST

Learn everything you can about the format (multiple choice, essay, etc.) and what will be on the test. Gather any study materials, course outlines, or sample exams that may be available. Not only will this help you to prepare, but knowing what to expect can help to alleviate test anxiety.

STEP 2: MAP OUT THE MATERIAL

Look through the textbook or study guide and make note of how many chapters or sections it has. Then divide these over the time you have. For example, if a book has 15 chapters and you have five days to study, you need to cover three chapters each day. Even better, if you have the time, leave an extra day at the end for overall review after you have gone through the material in depth.

If time is limited, you may need to prioritize the material. Look through it and make note of which sections you think you already have a good grasp on, and which need review. While you are studying, skim quickly through the familiar sections and take more time on the challenging parts.

Write out your plan so you don't get lost as you go. Having a written plan also helps you feel more in control of the study, so anxiety is less likely to arise from feeling overwhelmed at the amount to cover.

STEP 3: GATHER YOUR TOOLS

Decide what study method works best for you. Do you prefer to highlight in the book as you study and then go back over the highlighted portions? Or do you type out notes of the important information? Or is it helpful to make flashcards that you can carry with you? Assemble the pens, index cards, highlighters, post-it notes, and any other materials you may need so you won't be distracted by getting up to find things while you study.

If you're having a hard time retaining the information or organizing your notes, experiment with different methods. For example, try color-coding by subject with colored pens, highlighters, or post-it notes. If you learn better by hearing, try recording yourself reading your notes so you can listen while in the car, working out, or simply sitting at your desk. Ask a friend to quiz you from your flashcards, or try teaching someone the material to solidify it in your mind.

STEP 4: CREATE YOUR ENVIRONMENT

It's important to avoid distractions while you study. This includes both the obvious distractions like visitors and the subtle distractions like an uncomfortable chair (or a too-comfortable couch that makes you want to fall asleep). Set up the best study environment possible: good lighting and a comfortable work area. If background music helps you focus, you may want to turn it on, but otherwise keep the room quiet. If you are using a computer to take notes, be sure you don't have any other windows open, especially applications like social media, games, or anything else that could distract you. Silence your phone and turn off notifications. Be sure to keep water close by so you stay hydrated while you study (but avoid unhealthy drinks and snacks).

Also, take into account the best time of day to study. Are you freshest first thing in the morning? Try to set aside some time then to work through the material. Is your mind clearer in the afternoon or evening? Schedule your study session then. Another method is to study at the same time of day that you will take the test, so that your brain gets used to working on the material at that time and will be ready to focus at test time.

STEP 5: STUDY!

Once you have done all the study preparation, it's time to settle into the actual studying. Sit down, take a few moments to settle your mind so you can focus, and begin to follow your study plan. Don't give in to distractions or let yourself procrastinate. This is your time to prepare so you'll be ready to fearlessly approach the test. Make the most of the time and stay focused.

Of course, you don't want to burn out. If you study too long you may find that you're not retaining the information very well. Take regular study breaks. For example, taking five minutes out of every hour to walk briskly, breathing deeply and swinging your arms, can help your mind stay fresh.

As you get to the end of each chapter or section, it's a good idea to do a quick review. Remind yourself of what you learned and work on any difficult parts. When you feel that you've mastered the material, move on to the next part. At the end of your study session, briefly skim through your notes again.

But while review is helpful, cramming last minute is NOT. If at all possible, work ahead so that you won't need to fit all your study into the last day. Cramming overloads your brain with more information than it can process and retain, and your tired mind may struggle to recall even

138

previously learned information when it is overwhelmed with last-minute study. Also, the urgent nature of cramming and the stress placed on your brain contribute to anxiety. You'll be more likely to go to the test feeling unprepared and having trouble thinking clearly.

So don't cram, and don't stay up late before the test, even just to review your notes at a leisurely pace. Your brain needs rest more than it needs to go over the information again. In fact, plan to finish your studies by noon or early afternoon the day before the test. Give your brain the rest of the day to relax or focus on other things, and get a good night's sleep. Then you will be fresh for the test and better able to recall what you've studied.

STEP 6: TAKE A PRACTICE TEST

Many courses offer sample tests, either online or in the study materials. This is an excellent resource to check whether you have mastered the material, as well as to prepare for the test format and environment.

Check the test format ahead of time: the number of questions, the type (multiple choice, free response, etc.), and the time limit. Then create a plan for working through them. For example, if you have 30 minutes to take a 60-question test, your limit is 30 seconds per question. Spend less time on the questions you know well so that you can take more time on the difficult ones.

If you have time to take several practice tests, take the first one open book, with no time limit. Work through the questions at your own pace and make sure you fully understand them. Gradually work up to taking a test under test conditions: sit at a desk with all study materials put away and set a timer. Pace yourself to make sure you finish the test with time to spare and go back to check your answers if you have time.

After each test, check your answers. On the questions you missed, be sure you understand why you missed them. Did you misread the question (tests can use tricky wording)? Did you forget the information? Or was it something you hadn't learned? Go back and study any shaky areas that the practice tests reveal.

Taking these tests not only helps with your grade, but also aids in combating test anxiety. If you're already used to the test conditions, you're less likely to worry about it, and working through tests until you're scoring well gives you a confidence boost. Go through the practice tests until you feel comfortable, and then you can go into the test knowing that you're ready for it.

Test Tips

On test day, you should be confident, knowing that you've prepared well and are ready to answer the questions. But aside from preparation, there are several test day strategies you can employ to maximize your performance.

First, as stated before, get a good night's sleep the night before the test (and for several nights before that, if possible). Go into the test with a fresh, alert mind rather than staying up late to study.

Try not to change too much about your normal routine on the day of the test. It's important to eat a nutritious breakfast, but if you normally don't eat breakfast at all, consider eating just a protein bar. If you're a coffee drinker, go ahead and have your normal coffee. Just make sure you time it so that the caffeine doesn't wear off right in the middle of your test. Avoid sugary beverages, and drink enough water to stay hydrated but not so much that you need a restroom break 10 minutes into the

Mometrix

test. If your test isn't first thing in the morning, consider going for a walk or doing a light workout before the test to get your blood flowing.

Allow yourself enough time to get ready, and leave for the test with plenty of time to spare so you won't have the anxiety of scrambling to arrive in time. Another reason to be early is to select a good seat. It's helpful to sit away from doors and windows, which can be distracting. Find a good seat, get out your supplies, and settle your mind before the test begins.

When the test begins, start by going over the instructions carefully, even if you already know what to expect. Make sure you avoid any careless mistakes by following the directions.

Then begin working through the questions, pacing yourself as you've practiced. If you're not sure on an answer, don't spend too much time on it, and don't let it shake your confidence. Either skip it and come back later, or eliminate as many wrong answers as possible and guess among the remaining ones. Don't dwell on these questions as you continue—put them out of your mind and focus on what lies ahead.

Be sure to read all of the answer choices, even if you're sure the first one is the right answer. Sometimes you'll find a better one if you keep reading. But don't second-guess yourself if you do immediately know the answer. Your gut instinct is usually right. Don't let test anxiety rob you of the information you know.

If you have time at the end of the test (and if the test format allows), go back and review your answers. Be cautious about changing any, since your first instinct tends to be correct, but make sure you didn't misread any of the questions or accidentally mark the wrong answer choice. Look over any you skipped and make an educated guess.

At the end, leave the test feeling confident. You've done your best, so don't waste time worrying about your performance or wishing you could change anything. Instead, celebrate the successful completion of this test. And finally, use this test to learn how to deal with anxiety even better next time.

Review Video: Test Anxiety
Visit mometrix.com/academy and enter code: 100340

Important Qualification

Not all anxiety is created equal. If your test anxiety is causing major issues in your life beyond the classroom or testing center, or if you are experiencing troubling physical symptoms related to your anxiety, it may be a sign of a serious physiological or psychological condition. If this sounds like your situation, we strongly encourage you to seek professional help.

Additional Bonus Material

Due to our efforts to try to keep this book to a manageable length, we've created a link that will give you access to all of your additional bonus material:

mometrix.com/bonus948/keyalgebrai